PRAISE FOR
EDUHEROES

"Deanna Jump beautifully reminds us all that the most important part of teaching is forming relationships with our students, parents, and coworkers. In this book, she artfully weaves personal experiences with concrete examples that teach us all how to do the same. This book is a delight—just like Deanna is!"
—Kim Bearden, National Teachers Hall of Fame and cofounder of The Ron Clark Academy

"In *EduHeroes*, Deanna Jump truly catches lighting in a bottle. This book was just the jolt of energy I needed to keep walking this often difficult education path. Deanna provides easy takeaways wrapped up in heart. Once you pick up *EduHeroes*, you won't be able to put it down, and you'll find yourself coming back to it again and again."
—Todd Nesloney, TEPSA Director of Culture and Strategic Leadership and coauthor of *Kids Deserve It!*

"This book is just what my teacher heart needed to find my own inner eduhero! The stories are uplifting, and I connected with Deanna's triumphs, struggles, and heartbreak in the classroom. Thank you for writing a book that gives me the tools to strengthen my relationships in all aspects of teaching. Every teacher can benefit from this book!"
—Rachelle Smith, teacher and coauthor of *What the Teacher Wants* blog

"*EduHeroes* is exactly what new and seasoned teachers need to remember their why. Deanna believes every teacher has the power to make a difference in the lives of their students. She shares just how foundational relationships—with students, parents, teammates, administrators, and friends—are to a successful teacher. Thank you, Deanna, for always being inspiring, humble, and full of light and grace!"
—Abby Mullins, teacher and author of *Babbling Abby* blog

"I did not think it was possible for me to admire Deanna Jump more than I do, but this book has reminded me of all of the ways in which she is special. Deanna has added her creativity and experience to classrooms all over the world through her voice and ideas. Her advocacy for students and teachers shine throughout this book, and we are so blessed that she decided to share it with us all."
—Deedee Wills, teacher and author of *Mrs. Wills' Kindergarten* blog

"It's funny. You think you know someone because you follow them on social media or you've seen them on television or on stage. But it's not until you learn their full story that you fully grasp their immense impact, knowledge, and influence on the world. *EduHeroes* not only offers an authentic look at the inspirational life and successful teaching career of Deanna Jump but provides easy-to-implement classroom ideas and practical advice on building relationships and teams."
—Adam Dovico, author of *Inside the Trenches* and coauthor of *The Limitless School* and *When Kids Lead*

"Deanna's passion for encouraging students and educators radiates through every chapter of this book, as she shares personal stories and powerful strategies in order to help readers learn how to unleash their own eduhero powers to impact and inspire others. This book will help remind educators of all levels of experience what a positive impact they can make in their quest to truly change the world, one student at a time."
—Holly Ehle, teacher

"This book reassured me that I am doing everything I can to be an eduhero to each and every student of mine. This book is inspiring and encouraging to everyone in the education profession. 5 STARS!"
—Michael Newman, Texas kindergarten teacher

"Deanna Jump is a powerhouse of knowledge and a master of her craft. *EduHeroes* is about so much more than capes and spotlights. It's about becoming that one teacher who stays within a student's heart for years and years to come."
—Erin Kassly, teacher

EduHeroes

How to Transform Relationships Into Powerful Tools for Classroom Success

Deanna Jump

EduHeroes
© 2020 by Deanna Jump

All rights reserved. No part of this publication may be reproduced in any form or by any electronic or mechanical means, including information storage and retrieval systems, without permission in writing by the publisher, except by a reviewer who may quote brief passages in a review. For information regarding permission, contact the publisher at eduherobooking@gmail.com.

> This book is available at special discounts when purchased in quantity for use as premiums, promotions, fundraisers, or for educational use. For inquiries and details, contact the publisher at eduherobooking@gmail.com.

Published by DiggyPod.com
Tecumseh, MI
http://deannajump.com

Cover art by Michelle Tsivgadelis
Editing and Interior Design by My Writers' Connection

Library of Congress Control Number: 2020904044
Paperback ISBN: 978-1-7346869-0-6

First Printing: April 2020

CONTENTS

Foreword x

Why I Wrote This Book xiii

1: What Is an EduHero? 1

Section 1: Building Powerful Relationships 17

2: Our Primary Mission: Teacher-Student Relationships 19

3: Partners in Progress: The Teacher-Parent Relationship .. 37

4: Friends, Allies, and Supporters 51

Section 2: Harnessing the Power of the Team 65

5: EduHeroes Assemble! 67

Section 3: Unleashing Your EduHero Powers 81

6: What Changes Will Help Your Students Thrive? 85

7: EduHeroes Prepare for Greatness 93

8: EduHeroes Are Artists 101

9: EduHeroes Take Risks 113

10: EduHeroes are Lifelong Learners 119

11: Believe in Your EduHero Powers 125

12: Protect Your Superpowers 133

Moving Forward 141

Bibliography 145

About the Author 147

Thank you from the bottom of my heart.

Dedications can be so challenging because it takes a village to accomplish lifelong goals, and my EduHero Team consists of too many wonderful people to mention on a single page. I am truly blessed to be surrounded by people who ENCOURAGE and uplift me beyond belief.

I want to thank my second-grade teacher and first EduHero, Mrs. Schmidt, for showing me love, compassion, and kindness. But most of all, thank you for seeing me.

I owe so much gratitude to my husband, Ed, for rescuing me and showing me that I had the power to turn my life around and achieve my dreams.

I also want to thank my unbelievable family who support me in all my endeavors.

Finally, thank you to my former students, parents, and colleagues for all that you taught me and inspired in me.

~Deanna

FOREWORD

It's often said that *relationships are everything*, and for good reason. The universe is built on the nature of relationships—between stars and their planets, the interacting cells in our bodies, and the members of our families. Just as relationships make the difference in life, they have the power to significantly enhance what one can accomplish as an educator.

As a former teacher and current entrepreneur, I've seen firsthand how strong relationships have helped me in both the classroom and boardroom. This can be challenging for many of us in the field of education based on the widely diverse audience we interact with every day, but it is very much worth the effort.

Through thoughtful insights and well-tested strategies, Deanna Jump provides us with unique approaches for enhancing our classroom and community relationships. She knows what she's talking about! Deanna has been instrumental in building relationships among

Paul Edelman founder of Teachers Pay Teachers with Deanna Jump

educators worldwide through the sharing of ideas and best practices. With more than twenty years of classroom teaching and a penchant for bringing people together, Deanna provides us with exciting strategies to make lasting impressions in our students' lives. She reminds us of the positive impact we can make as educators in the classroom, school, and community—and how better relationships make everything we do more powerful.

I highly encourage you to read this inspiring book and share with others around you. Create your own EduHero team and revolutionize your practice!

Paul Edelman
former NYC middle school teacher
founder of Teachers Pay Teachers

WHY I WROTE THIS BOOK

I have been blessed with the opportunity to converse with thousands of teachers each year through Get Your Teach On conferences, *Teachers Pay Teachers*, blog meetups, online forums, and, of course, classroom observations. The passion, enthusiasm, and energy that teachers willingly put forth every day in their classrooms to make an impact on their students' lives never fails to inspire and impress me.

Teachers face numerous obstacles on a daily basis. We must overcome these challenges to ensure our students obtain the best education possible. Our time both inside and outside the classroom is limited, which is why this book has been several years in the making. If you're anything like me, you understand that teaching is a calling versus a career choice. Being an educator can overshadow other aspects of our lives, like finding the time to write a book!

But I knew I needed to pass along the insights I've gained from the stories and experiences so many teachers have shared with me throughout my twenty-plus years of teaching and presenting. My career has provided me with a great vantage point of this ever-changing and ever-challenging world of education. I've learned, for instance, that although our educational system is far from perfect, relationships between students and teachers, administrators, and staff are the vital links that can close the gap between student achievement and failure. Building strong, substantial relationships is the cornerstone for our success as educators. I've also learned that open lines of communication and straightforward, honest dialogue can lead to amazing accomplishments within any school. Most importantly, I've seen firsthand that when we refuse to limit our beliefs about our potential impact as educators—when we truly unleash our superpowers—we can change the world one student at a time.

My ultimate goal for this book is for you to become a superhero teacher, equipped with powers of encouragement, passion, caring—both in and out of the classroom—and the ability to fly. (Okay, maybe not fly. But wouldn't that be helpful for getting to school on time?) Throughout this book, I'll share insights to building stronger relationships within your unique educational community. We'll dive into strategies for establishing stronger lines of communications with students, parents, administrators, and others we touch on a daily basis. And you'll uncover your unique superpowers and unleash your full potential as the best kind of superhero: an *EduHero*.

I know my goals may sound somewhat unrealistic, especially in light of the challenges you and your colleagues may be facing, but I believe the only way to succeed is to set and strive for big goals. So let's put on our capes and start the journey together!

1

WHAT IS AN EDUHERO?

Children may not remember what you taught them, but they will always remember how you made them feel.
—Maya Angelou

If you've kept up with the superhero movie craze, you can probably list the various superpowers and traits of the most popular fictional heroes.

- Faster than a locomotive
- Able to leap small buildings in a single bound
- X-ray vision
- Superhuman strength
- The ability to teleport

Even one or two of these superhuman powers would make life so much easier. I know I'm not suddenly going to develop the ability to blink myself to Paris, but a girl can dream!

As an EduHero, you may never possess superhuman powers, but it isn't exaggerating to say the impact you make could inspire new dreams within a child or even save his or her life. That's how we change the world.

Ordinary educators perform their daily activities with a focus on teaching the standards and just getting through the day. They look forward to leaving school as soon as the final bell rings. Survival is their best hope. They escape each day with little thought or effort expended on building relationships or planning future lessons.

Before you think that I'm throwing these survivalist teachers under the bus, let me say that everyone—including me—has taken the "duck-and-cover" approach to teaching from time to time. I can remember a time when I had a kindergarten class consisting of nineteen boys and five girls. My classroom management style that year resembled that of a referee with the

World Wrestling Federation, only I was on the losing end of the match. If I turned my back for a moment, chaos would soon ensue. The way I felt that year reminds me of the scene in the movie *Kindergarten Cop* when Arnold Schwarzenegger, in the role of Detective John Kimble, falls face first onto the bed, exhausted and beaten down, after just one day of teaching a kindergarten class. Teaching is not for the faint of heart. As Kimble discovered, students can sense fear, and unprepared, unorganized teachers will struggle to simply survive. My main goal was to simply survive this classroom—when what it really needed was an EduHero.

An EduHero is an educator who is passionate about teaching children and who views his or her role as a calling, rather than just a job. To be an EduHero, you must embrace that calling with enthusiasm, compassion, commitment, and sincerity. More than that, the commitment must be to the whole child—from the academic progress to the emotional, physical, and social well-being of each unique individual in your care.

> **Ordinary educators** follow the instructional plan. They teach the same things the same way to every student, year after year.
>
> **EduHeroes** provide their students with opportunities to learn and apply skills in a meaningful context. It is important for students to realize that they are capable learners, that they can make choices, and that their ideas are respected and valued.
>
> **Ordinary educators** don't get involved. They're there to teach. End of story.

An EduHero is an educator who is passionate about teaching children and who views his or her role as a calling, rather than just a job.

What Is an EduHero?

EduHeroes believe children should leave school each day feeling better about themselves than when they walked in the classroom. These educators are willing to go out of their way to make a positive lasting impact on a student's life. EduHeroes will strive to build strong relationships to overcome any obstacles they encounter. These relationships help them better understand each student's unique abilities and needs, and they prioritize those needs rather than prioritizing the curriculum.

It's interesting to note that once Detective John Kimball began asking questions about his students and their families (although he had an ulterior motive), he slowly began to build and establish relationships with his students. The focus on building relationships turned his chaotic classroom into a place where students could learn and thrive.

ENCOURAGE and believe in your students and yourself!

All superheroes have a motto or philosophy for which they stand. Superman's comes to mind: "Truth, justice, and the American way!" Well, EduHeroes should also have a motto (or maybe just an acronym) to live by, and here's mine: ENCOURAGE.

ENGAGE your students by making the learning memorable and meaningful.

NURTURE your students' creativity. Provide opportunities for them to play, work on projects, and solve problems creatively. Encourage them to take risks and learn from their failures. STEM projects are a great place to start!

COMPASSION must be modeled on a daily basis. Show kindness and empathy. Take the time to understand other perspectives.

OPEN up to let your students know you are a real person who cares about their well-being, both in and out of the classroom.

UPLIFT your students every day. Always praise your students publicly and discipline in private.

RESPECT has to be earned. If you want your students to respect you, you must first respect them.

ATTENTION should be given to your students with the emphasis on two-way communication. Getting your students' attention and maintaining their interest can take many forms. I'll share some of my favorite attention-getting strategies later.

GREATNESS! Look for greatness in your students. When you see it, say it! There are no limits to the amount of praise that we can give our students. One kind word or gesture can make a world of difference and lead to greatness.

EMPOWER your students to reach higher. Give your students a voice. Provide them with multiple opportunities to share their thinking and collaborate with others. Let them know that all thinking is valued.

My Backstory

A superhero is defined as a fictional character endowed with superhuman powers who is usually portrayed as fighting evil or crime. But that isn't the only definition. What if I told you each and every one of us is capable of being a superhero? That's because the true definition of a superhero is someone who makes a lasting positive impact on another person's life. My second-grade teacher fit the latter description. She was my superhero—my EduHero. And because of the impact she had on my life, I grew up and became an EduHero just like her.

Me, Second Grade

All superheroes have a backstory. Let me tell you mine.

I was born into a family plagued with generational alcohol and child abuse. My mother was married nine times by the time I entered fourth grade, but not one of those marriages was to my father. In fact, my father didn't

Kids who need love the most often ask for it in the most unloving ways.

even know about me until I was sixteen years old. We lived in a constant state of upheaval as we moved around from place to place. It was fairly common for us to move during the middle of the school year, which meant the only consistent part of school for me during my early education years was the fact that everything was constantly new—new schools, new teachers, new classmates.

The saying, "Kids who need love the most often ask for it in the most unloving ways," isn't just a popular meme to share. It's the truth. And that hard truth didn't make me a class favorite. In kindergarten and first grade, I spent quite a bit of time sitting by myself in the hall during class time and standing next to the fence at recess. My teachers viewed me as a behavior problem and a child seeking attention. They failed to understand that my home life induced trauma and I lacked the appropriate skills to deal with it. I wasn't seeking attention. I was seeking a connection. At home I longed to be invisible, but at school I just wanted to be seen.

Then Mrs. Schmidt, my second-grade teacher, stepped into my story. At first glance she looked just like any other teacher, but Mrs. Schmidt had a superpower. She had x-ray vision, and she saw through the bad behavior. She knew that reading, writing, and math skills weren't what I needed most from her. She understood (without me having to tell her) that I just needed to know someone cared about me—that I was worthy. Each day she greeted me with a warm smile and told me she was happy to see me. She was consistent, fair, and always looked for greatness in her students. She took the time to make a connection. Her compassion and understanding equipped me with the social skills I needed to flourish.

In the spring of my second-grade year, my mom told me we were moving yet again. I remember tearfully telling Mrs. Schmidt that I wouldn't be back the following day. She gave me a hug that seemed to last for an eternity, a hug that lasted so long her heart seemed to speak to mine. It was a hug I will always remember. As she hugged me, she told me that no matter where I was in the world, she would be thinking of me and she knew I was capable of great things. Because of the impact she had on my life, I eventually defied what statistics said I should have been.

Every child needs a superhero, and Mrs. Schmidt was mine. The love and guidance she provided me that year made a permanent impact on my life. Her cape was invisible, but her words and actions were powerful.

Fast forward to high school. Desperate to escape my dysfunctional home life, I got married at sixteen. I thought marriage would bring a sense of normalcy and steadiness to my life. Quitting high school, working two jobs to get by, and failing at a teenage marriage turned out to be my harsh reality. My insecurities and situation seemed insurmountable, but Mrs. Schmidt's words never left me. I knew I was capable of so much more. And honestly, deep down, I wanted her to be proud of me, wherever she was. I knew I wasn't going to be bitten by a radioactive spider, so I had to strap on my work boots and get busy being the person she ENCOURAGED me to be.

I worked hard to earn my GED and spent several years as a home daycare provider, watching ten-plus children ranging in age from two to five, while attending college part-time. This was challenging to say the least, but I had discovered my calling. I wanted to teach. I eventually completed my bachelor's degree and began my teaching career. It wasn't too long into my first year of teaching that I realized I was not prepared to be a teacher.

Finding My Balance as an EduHero

How often do you think, *If I only had a couple more hours, I could* _____*?* I bet you could fill in the blank with numerous things. It is truly amazing how teachers seem to find the time to complete so many tasks during a normal school day. Very few professions have such a regimented schedule where each teaching period, bathroom break, lunchtime, or planning meeting is broken down to the very minute! It can be difficult for any one person to stay on such a tight schedule, and when you add twenty-plus children into the equation, staying on track can become extremely challenging.

For the most part, teachers take each day in stride and find a way to accommodate these tight schedules and deadlines every day, but if you're like many educators, you wonder often: ***How can I balance all of these requirements effectively while maintaining my sanity?!*** Let's not forget, we are also seeking to find some quality time for our personal lives outside the classroom.

When I was a new teacher twenty-plus years ago, I constantly had a sinking feeling that came from not being able to manage my time and responsibilities well. Maybe that's where you are now as you struggle to juggle classroom management, duties before and after school, grading, and preparations for class tomorrow, all the while wishing you had more time to individually evaluate your students so you can better understand their needs. Each day comes with new challenges, and sometimes you feel completely overwhelmed. I remember that stress as if it were yesterday!

As a first year first-grade teacher at Ruskin Elementary, I was terrified of trying to teach my students to read and write for the first time. I felt ill equipped due to the lack of training provided by my university. I had memorized all of the key vocabulary, passed all the tests with flying colors, but did I truly know how to teach? No!

It is an understatement to say I wasn't prepared for my first full-time teaching job. Ruskin Elementary was a Title I school with a large student population of migrant farmworker households. Multiple languages were spoken within the classroom. I didn't have any training in ESL (English as a second language) strategies, nor did I fully understand some of the cultures and backgrounds of my students. In hindsight, I probably could have done several things differently, but reflection is easier when you are not in over your head! What I learned from my first year of teaching was that I needed to first educate myself on the ins and outs of teaching and building relationships, as well as educate myself on the diverse cultures represented in my school and community. It was through that process of desperate self-education that I discovered my passion for creating engaging lessons and developing relationships with all of my students, and those passions continue to grow to this day. Even though I feel much better equipped today to handle the challenges that come with teaching, I constantly seek out strategies to improve student engagement and to understand why relationships matter.

During every Get Your Teach On conference, teachers approach me with the same question I asked all those years ago as a new teacher: How is it possible to fit everything in and still maintain some sense of balance throughout the day? My answer is straightforward: You must discard things that have little impact on your students and focus on what is most important. Being intentional with your time, planning, and classroom instruction will make it possible to successfully manage the juggling act. Don't get me wrong: We all have days that seem like nothing goes according to plan, but when we teach with intention, we can make those days the exceptions rather than the norm.

As part of that intention, we must plan our classroom day with a focus on ENCOURAGE-ing student success. We can do that best when we know our students and their needs, which means the place to begin this epic journey is with a focus on *relationships*.

NOTES

Section 1

BUILDING POWERFUL RELATIONSHIPS

WHY DID YOU BECOME A TEACHER? Was it the high pay, short workdays, or the long summer vacations?

Just kidding! Now that you've stopped rolling your eyes and can focus on the page again, take a few minutes to think about the moment you decided to become a teacher.

I don't remember the exact moment I knew I wanted to be a teacher, but I know that my second-grade teacher, Mrs. Schmidt, was my inspiration. I wanted to have a positive impact on students' lives, just as she'd had on mine. I'm still working toward fulfilling that goal. (It's a lifelong pursuit for me!)

My assumption—because you are reading this book—is that you want to make a positive impact on others' lives too. Your goal (or at least one of them) is to help people succeed, whether that's in school, at work, at home, in life, or all of the above. To accomplish that mission, you have to know your students and their families. You have to *know* your colleagues. It's through strong relationships that we can make the greatest difference.

Let's start this section by exploring a few ways to nurture our most important relationship: the teacher-student relationship.

2

OUR PRIMARY MISSION: TEACHER-STUDENT RELATIONSHIPS

No man stands so tall as when he stoops to help a child.
—Abraham Lincoln

Before You Begin This Chapter, Let's Do a Quick **EDUHERO** Reflection

What kind of relationships do you have with your students?

- Friendly
- Positive
- Meaningful
- Powerful
- Constructive
- Frustrating
- Impersonal
- Negative
- Antagonistic
- _____

What are you satisfied or happy about regarding your relationships with students?

What would you like to change or improve about your relationships with your students?

What will you to do make that change?

Our Primary Mission: Teacher-Student Relationships

The relationship between teacher and students is critically important to how well students learn. In his research, Robert Marzano found that positive relationships between students and teachers are among the most commonly cited variables associated with effective instruction.[1] Strong relationships increase student motivation, improve student achievement, and greatly reduce behavioral issues.

Our most important job as teachers is to make sure we get to know our students, show respect for their culture, and connect with them on a meaningful level. It is through relationship building that we learn how to meet students' needs and teach and treat each child as an individual. With that in mind, be intentional about establishing a meaningful relationship with each and every student as soon as possible each school year.

A great place to start is with your class list. Prior to the beginning of the school year, we all receive our student classroom list. This list is our starting point for relationship building. Send each student a postcard or even an email or text. Make sure to address your note to the student, not the parent (we will talk about the parents later). A friend of mine sends a letter to her students telling them a little bit about herself. What makes this letter special, and a little more personal, is that she adds a QR code. The link leads to a recording of a personal voice message where she tells the students a little more information about herself and shares some of the exciting things they will be doing in first grade. This initial communication doesn't have to be lengthy; just let them know you look forward to meeting them and can't wait to see them soon.

Strong relationships increase student motivation, improve student achievement, and greatly reduce behavioral issues.

Give Them a Fresh Start

I know that some years, the shear shock of seeing your classroom makeup for the first time can throw you for a loop. (Remember when I told you about the year I had nineteen boys and five girls? That list was certainly shocking!) Other times, you might see the name of a rumored "problem child" on your class list and instantly feel cold chills run down your spine. But I want to offer a word of caution: When you get your class list, do your best to avoid making assumptions about your incoming students. It's common for teachers to talk about their past students, particularly those who were challenging. If you allow your perception of students to develop negatively, based on what another teacher says, you do those students and yourself a disservice. Your perceptions may well turn out to be inaccurate misperceptions, and it can be very difficult for you to build a meaningful relationship if you have preconceived notions about the student. If a colleague starts telling you about all the behavioral problems she had with a particular student, stop her. Change the topic or simply make up an excuse to disengage from the conversation. Yes, teachers need to be aware of academic and health challenges, but behavior problems are another issue for several reasons. Often, all the child needs is a fresh start.

A couple of years ago, my daughter Taylor was a first-year teacher at a relatively small school in central Florida. I was blessed to be given the opportunity to teach next door to Taylor and was able to assist her whenever necessary. Because the school was small, teachers tended to know about other students in the school, especially the ones deemed challenging. During a teacher planning meeting, several teachers jokingly told

Taylor they would pray for her because Jake* was on her class list (*name changed to protect the innocent). They went on to describe Jake and his challenges, and by the time they were done, they had told her more than she wanted to know.

Taylor, however, believes as I do that each and every student deserves an opportunity for a fresh start and a clean slate. Jake was indeed a very challenging student. Even so, Taylor made sure to tell him she was happy he was in her class. His little face lit up, and it was obvious that he had never heard those words before. Taylor worked with Jake, got to know him, and strove to encourage him. She watched for things to compliment him on and told him every time she saw greatness in him. The way she lovingly and naturally took care to nurture Jake's needs made me so proud.

At the end of the year, I decided to have the kids create a special book for Taylor to commemorate her first year as a teacher. The book was titled "My Favorite Part of First Grade,"

Taylor and I starting our journey as co-teachers

If our most challenging students are made to feel like they are our favorite students, we have truly made a difference.

and Jake's contribution brought tears to my eyes. His page said, "My favorite part of first grade was being Mrs. Miller's favorite student."

I wanted to know exactly what his thought process was, so I asked him to tell me more about it. "What makes you think you were Mrs. Miller's favorite?" I asked.

He replied, "She always asked me to sit by her on the carpet."

You see, Taylor not only had great classroom management, but she also knew the importance of building children up, making them feel special, and creating meaningful connections. She was proactive rather than reactive. She invited Jake to sit by her to avoid any potential behavior problems. This simple gesture made him feel special and made him feel as if he were her favorite.

Think of some of the challenging students you've had in the past. Did you ENCOURAGE them? Did you give them the opportunity to have a fresh start each and every day? Did you look for and focus on the positive, or did you dwell on the negative? If our most challenging students are made to feel like they are our favorite students, we have truly made a difference.

Get on Their Level

It is my belief that we should teach students on their eye level rather than towering above them. We have always been taught that making eye contact with an audience is vital for establishing meaningful relationships. This holds true in your classroom as well. Students seek connections with their teacher, and direct eye contact is a great place to start. It may take a little extra effort to accomplish this goal, but it's well worth it. As a kindergarten and first-grade teacher, this means I am constantly

Get on their level

bending, kneeling, or sitting next to my students throughout the school day. When I teach a lesson, I bring the students in close to me on the teaching carpet whenever possible. My teacher chair sits low to the floor so I can maintain eye contact. Don't elevate yourself above your students; reach out to them on their level. Teachers want their students to achieve greater things in life, so start the journey beside them, not above them!

    I recently watched a documentary about Mr. Rodgers and his impact on children's lives over several decades. One of my takeaways from his story was his ability to build meaningful relationships with children. It was important to notice how he talked "with" children on their level, face-to-face, with kindness and compassion in his heart. His demeanor and gentle nature taught a generation of kids the value of kindness. Teachers can learn from these small gestures in the classroom. It can be challenging for teachers to constantly maintain face-to-face contact, but face-to-face contact is important, as it helps us gauge

To be an EduHero, we have to use our super listening skills!

whether or not our students are actively listening and understanding the lesson. Keep in mind there are various reasons some of your students may avoid eye contact (for example, students of other cultures, those who have been diagnosed with Autism Spectrum Disorder, and students who have experienced trauma). Making eye contact and engaging in face-to-face interactions helps establish secure relationships between teachers and students.

My son, Hunter, played college basketball at a small Christian university. His best friend, A.J., is a towering seven foot one. Standing next to A.J., Hunter at six feet tall looks short in comparison. It was interesting to observe A.J. talking to children at

A.J. and Hunter

basketball games or out in public. Even though it was awkward and physically uncomfortable, A.J. didn't hesitate to bend down and talk to children. Their faces always lit up when he got down on their level. My point is that we must make the same effort with our students. They will appreciate the gesture!

Greet Them Every Day

In his book *The First Days of School: How to Be an Effective Teacher*, Harry Wong states, "Greeting students will have the most immediate impact on your day."[2] It begins at the door, and a greeting every morning is the first step in making a positive connection. I know it can be a chaotic time prior to the first morning bell, but this small gesture will help start the day off on the right foot. Please don't make this a generic greeting with little effort or enthusiasm; your students will notice! Pay attention and comment on the small things, like a haircut or new shoes. You don't need a fancy handshake or dance move; you just need to make sure your students know you see them and you are happy they are there.

Get Personal

Work at getting to know your students better throughout the year. Do you know your students' backstories? Do you know what makes them happy, sad, scared, or excited? Which students do you need to know better? Get personal and ask your students about themselves, their families, interests, and hobbies. Be prepared to hear some interesting stories in response! If you are like me, it may be necessary to write a few notes to remember their stories, especially at the beginning of the school year.

Our Primary Mission: Teacher-Student Relationships

Even if your students seem tight-lipped at the start of the school year, it's only a matter of time before they become comfortable sharing their stories once they know you care.

Use Your Super Listening Skills

Mrs. Schmidt taught me that "active listening" can be a superpower, if consistently used in the classroom. How would you describe your listening skills? I've been guilty at times of focusing so much on teaching that I forgot to actually listen to my students. It's so easy to become laser focused on the learning outcomes that we forget our students also need non-academic attention. To be an EduHero, we have to use our super listening skills!

Speak to Uplift

A close acquaintance of mine taught in an inner-city Title I elementary school. Being able to visit and teach various special lessons and complete several room transformations throughout the year for her first-grade class was a treat for me. Her students always seemed so excited and eager to learn. The school was beautifully decorated with student work displayed throughout the hallways. It was obvious that teachers took pride in their jobs; however, there was something missing.

One of the things I noticed when visiting the school was the prevalence of teachers "barking" commands at their students in the hallways, cafeteria, and inside the classroom. The school atmosphere felt very tense, with an emphasis given to maintaining total control over the students, regardless of the situation. The philosophy that "a child should be seen, not heard" fit well within this school. It made me very uncomfortable whenever I witnessed this behavior toward students. Let me step in here and say that I have taught at Title I schools, and I know there are many challenges teachers face. Teaching is hard. Teaching in poverty is even harder. It is a common misconception that the educators who teach in Title I schools are the worst. This is so untrue! Most teachers in these schools are there because they are passionate about education and want to help all kids succeed. Passionate teachers know these kids don't need teachers to be tougher on them simply because they attend an inner-city school. It is important that we take time to understand the issues these students face and treat them with kindness and compassion.

Regardless of where you teach, kids are kids. Whether you teach in an affluent school, an urban school, or an inner-city school, you will have students who have experienced trauma; these students will find a barrage of commands or harsh tones to be especially triggering. Reduce the possibility of causing stress or anxiety by using a calm voice, being respectful, and creating a dialogue with your students. Remember, it's hard to see the greatness in your students when they aren't given the opportunity to express themselves.

If someone were to overhear you talking to your students, what assumptions might they make about you as a teacher? Can you think of positive, constructive ways to encourage your students to reach new heights? Remember, it's important to set high expectations for your students, but it is equally important to nurture mutual respect. Speak to uplift using words that tell students you value them. Positive words are some of your most effective superpowers!

Set Reasonable Expectations and Be Consistent

Classroom management is an important aspect of creating an effective learning environment. Setting expectations and defining procedures are essential. It is equally important, however, to think about the individual students in the classrooms when setting those expectations. I can think of a number of students who couldn't sit still no matter how hard they tried. In order for them to be able to focus on the lesson and not interrupt the learning of others, I had to accommodate their needs and allow them the space to move around during the lesson.

In her book *Fostering Resilient Learners,* Kristen Souers states that if a behavior is predictable, it's preventable.[3] This means that for some students you may need to analyze their behaviors and look for stressors that are predictable so you can put some interventions in place to help them successfully work through the behaviors. Each student has different needs, both academically and behaviorally. We differentiate instruction based on academic needs, but oftentimes we overlook the need to differentiate based on behavior. Even as you accommodate for each student's learning styles, be consistent with the rules and expectations so that students know what is expected of them. Hold students accountable for their learning and let them know you believe in them.

Be consistent and follow through. When you follow through with what you have said you are going to do, your students learn that they can trust you and that you won't let them down. School may be the only place where they can feel a sense of stability, and your consistency provides security for them.

Smile!

Don't forget to smile. Take the time to laugh with your class as often as possible. Share funny stories about yourself and let your students tell their stories. It is important for your students to view you as a compassionate and caring person who wants them to succeed in all aspects of life. Please don't assume that smiling, laughing, and sharing with your class means you won't be able to have effective classroom management. In fact, the opposite effect will occur when students feel connected to you. In her TED Talk, Rita Pierson stated, "Kids don't learn from teachers they don't like."[4] I agree 100 percent!

Be Positive

We all experience terrible days—mornings where we overslept, our car wouldn't start, or we had an argument with our spouse. Everyone goes through personal trials that can be

Full hands, full heart

difficult to handle. However, it is imperative that once we step into the classroom, we leave those problems behind so they don't interfere with our ability to teach or impede relationship building with our students. Teachers should approach their classroom each day with a positive attitude. Just take a deep breath and focus on what you do best. Be a caring, compassionate encourager. Positivity is contagious, and we must lead by example.

Hug (or High-Five or Fist Bump) Them Back!

How do you respond if students try to hug you? I know some teachers are always ready with a hug in return. Others feel awkward with any physical contact whatsoever. If that's you, the next time a student leans in for a hug, ask yourself, "What is this child seeking?" It could be love, attention, comfort, or connection.

As a kindergarten and first-grade teacher, my reaction to student-initiated physical contact has always been to respond in kind. I am always ready with a hug, high-five, or fist bump! Sometimes the hug you give a student might be the only one they receive that day. You may not agree with me, but I believe it is important for us to make a connection with our students and let them know we care about them. Sometimes physical connection is what students need the most. If they initiate a hug and you tell them no, they will see that as a rejection, and it can shatter the relationship you've taken the time to build.

Teach with Your Heart

Allow yourself the opportunity to let your heart lead the way. Your passion and love for teaching should show in the way you interact with your students and encourage them to reach their fullest potential. It is easy to coast along in cruise-control mode, especially late in the school year. I ENCOURAGE you to finish strong and leave a lasting impression of love and compassion with your students. These are memorable times for them and us. So reach down deep, roll up your sleeves, and teach with all your heart!

Love your students. Cheer for them. Look for the greatness in them and let them know what you see in them!

Look for the greatness in your students and let them know what you see in them!

FANTASTIC FOUR TAKEAWAYS

1 Speak to your students as if someone else were listening in.

2 Great classroom management starts with establishing mutual respect.

3 Get personal; Take the time to listen and get to know your students.

4 Remember a one-size-fits-all approach doesn't work! Be consistent and set reasonable expectations that are unique to each student.

3

PARTNERS IN PROGRESS: THE TEACHER-PARENT RELATIONSHIP

Alone we can do so little,
together we can do so much.
—Helen Keller

Our job is to educate children, and parents play a vital role in this process. Experts agree that parent involvement in education is one of the biggest predictors of student success. According to a report in *NEA Today*, "Family engagement in schools improves student achievement, reduces absenteeism, and restores parents' confidence in their children's education."[1] As teachers, we can all share stories of having some challenging parents over the years. I would encourage you not to view parents as villains but as a part of your EduHero team. It may take time to get your students' parents on board, but when they are working with you, your students will benefit. When parents and teachers form a partnership, it sends a message to students that education is valued and lets them know they have a strong, consistent team of people who want to help them succeed. The following are a few ways to get parents on your EduHero team.

Be Intentional with Your First Contact

Teacher-parent relationships can take many forms based on undefined expectations by both parties. In my career, I've seen overly dominant, helicopter parents who hover over their children, as well as parents on the opposite end of the spectrum who are completely removed from their children's educational success. Regardless of where parents fall in their involvement, I have found it is important for teachers to create open lines of communications as quickly as possible.

For many parents, the first interaction they have with the school each year is the supply list that is posted around the school, online, and at the local Walmart. Is this the first communication you want with parents? Don't get me wrong—teachers need classroom supplies, but can't we be a little more proactive with our first impressions with parents? A quick email, text, postcard, or even a brief phone call to introduce yourself can create open lines of communications before the kick off of the new school year. Reaching out in this way is a great start for building a meaningful relationship with parents. Establishing a rapport with parents early on will not only help ease the sticker shock of the school supply list but also open the dialogue for other assistance around the classroom. You can never have enough volunteers, right?

Define Roles and Expectations

It's common to hear recommendations about "managing expectations," but this is not an easy task since every student is unique in their educational and personal needs. But it can be easy to establish some very specific learning and behavioral expectations for everyone. It's important to clearly communicate everyone's role and expectations for student success. I have found that parents are very receptive when I describe my own expectations and responsibilities as a teacher, along with my teaching philosophies to promote and encourage their child's success. The two most important things you can do for your students this year is to ENCOURAGE and believe in them. I have yet to have a parent argue with this teaching philosophy. As an EduHero, it is important to avoid playing the blame game where everyone is looking to pass responsibility for educational success to someone else. It's a team effort!

Communicate Clearly and Appropriately

Sending written notes home with students isn't always the most effective way to communicate with parents. In some (many) cases, those notes get buried in students' backpacks or lunch boxes and never reach the intended recipient. On the flip side, while technology can be a wonderful thing, a text message with five different emojis to communicate a child's challenge in class may not be effective (or appropriate) either.

Regardless of the delivery of your message, the tone, sense of urgency, or even the timing of the message can be misinterpreted. One way to ensure effective communication is to be consistent and to vary the ways you reach out to parents. Phone calls and in-person meetings may seem to take more time, but they are also the best way to ensure your message is received as intended.

A class blog would be a great way to provide a virtual window into your classroom. You can showcase student work, highlight things you are doing in your classroom and keep parents up to date on what their child is learning. Worried about finding the time? Have the students help write the content and take pictures for the post. This would be a great way to teach digital citizenship and incorporate authentic writing in your classroom.

Make the Most of Parent-Teacher Conferences

Parent-teacher conferences provide the opportunity for face-to-face interactions that ensure everyone is on the same

Phone calls and in-person meetings may seem to take more time, but they are also the best way to ensure your message is received as intended.

page and moving in the right direction. They can be an excellent time for building relationships with parents. They can also be a little unnerving, especially for new teachers.

The keys to making the most of this valuable time are to organize your thoughts and message prior to meeting with parents, maintain a positive attitude, and be prepared to listen. Before the meeting, define your expectations and goals, but keep in mind that these meetings are a two-way street. Make sure to allow parents the opportunity to talk, and while they're talking, use your superpowers to listen. You may learn something new and interesting or get a completely different perspective on your students and their perception of school—and you. I have always tried to keep these three Cs in mind when meeting with parents: caring, compassion, and conversation.

One of my favorite stories about a parent-teacher meeting involves the first parent-teacher conference Taylor had with Jake's dad. Jake's dad came alone to the conference, and before Taylor could start, he said, "I want you to know what a difference you have made in Jake. He loves school, and he gets ready each morning without a fight. Last year he had to be dragged out of bed each morning, forced to get dressed, and when we drove up in the carpool line it usually took three adults to wrestle him out of the car. My wife and I couldn't understand why he disliked school so much.

"We knew he was challenging for the teacher, and we received evidence of that almost every day via a note or phone call home. But we kept trying to support the teacher and trying everything we knew to help Jake with his behavior. When we entered the kindergarten room for the first parent-teacher conference, the teacher wasn't there. We casually walked around the room looking at the student work and charts. I witnessed my wife's heart break that day. You see, without a word from his teacher, we were finally able to fully understand why Jake disliked school. There on the wall was a bright chart with all of the students' names going vertically down the side. Next to each student's name were lots of brightly colored smiley-faced stickers. Every student, that is, except Jake. After forty-five days of school, he didn't have one single sticker. Not one. So many questions we had were answered by that single chart. Jake disliked school because his teacher disliked him."

Let me jump in here. I know there are times that students test you and make you question your choice of professions on a daily basis. Believe me, I've been there and, like I shared in my backstory, I was that student. As educators we have to make sure we aren't always focusing on the negative behaviors. When we focus on the negative, that may become all we see. Use your superpowers. Look at each child and find the good in them. When you see it, let them know. ENCOURAGE and uplift your students. Don't misunderstand me: I'm definitely not saying that you should overlook all negative behavior. What I'm saying is, make sure there is a balance. Always start the year with positive communication. Parents notice, and what they notice can either make them a supportive part of your EduHero team or make them an adversary. EduHeroes should have short-term memory loss. When it comes to student behaviors, we must be willing to allow our students a fresh start each day. Focus on the present, not past, behaviors. You owe it to yourself, your students, and their parents. Use your team and seek the assistance of others, especially parents. Remember, they are a vital part of your EduHero team.

We must be willing to allow our students a fresh start each day.

Encourage Parent Involvement

Parental involvement in your classroom plays a vital role in student success. Encouraging parents to participate in various classroom activities gives parents a chance to become an active participant in their child's education. Being involved will create a sense of pride and ownership for them. Are there specific activities you have implemented throughout the year to increase parent involvement? Below are a few examples of events that have worked for me in gaining parent participation.

- **Parent Night**—When I was at Quail Run Elementary (QRE), my team realized that parents didn't understand what a day in the life of their kindergarten student looked like. They heard terms like "Guided Reading and Writers Workshop," but they had no idea what they meant. My team and I wanted to be able to show them what their children were doing during each part of the school day, so we took pictures and developed a slide show that broke down each part of the schedule and explained the instructional focus. We invited the parents to join us for this special gathering so we could share the information with them. The hour we spent made a huge impact on the relationship with parents because it allowed them to understand what a day inside our classrooms looked like. Our parent volunteer list exploded because parents wanted to be part of the learning process.

- **Gingerbread Man Play** (think reader's theater on steroids)—December lessons typically include a variety of gingerbread stories. One year, I found a Gingerbread Man musical play from Heidi Butkus. The first year our class performed the play, we used simple paper headbands and paper props for decorations. After we practiced for a few weeks, we invited the parents to attend our play and decorate gingerbread houses afterwards. The event was so successful and the parents loved it so much that I decided to take it a step further the following year. I enlisted the help of our high school drama department to build a more elaborate set. We held a performance during the school day and once again decorated gingerbread houses with parents after our performance. We then held two additional showings in the evening because we had so many grandparents, aunts, and uncles who wanted to attend.

I know what some of you are thinking: *Ain't nobody got time for that!* But the impact speaks for itself: All of my students were excited to play a part in the performance, and their parents are still talking about it years later.

Gingerbread Man bridge

Gingerbread Man play

- **Literacy Night**—This was a school-wide event that parents and students were invited to attend. We covered the school walls with displays of student work and stationed literacy games and activities throughout the school for the parents and students to do together. Our focus was to provide parents with an opportunity to learn a variety of ways to support their child's learning at home. This was so successful that we followed the same model a few months later and hosted a school-wide Math Mania.

EduHeroes

- **Pirates and Pizza**—The end of the year is exhausting and chaotic, but I believe in finishing just as strongly as we begin. Our last unit of study for the year is Ocean Animals. For our literature study, we added in the fiction story, "How I Became a Pirate." The kids learned the "Pirate Song" from *The Backyardigans*, and we made simple pirate costumes. We displayed the student work from our unit of study throughout the room and invited parents in for an afternoon of Pirates and Pizza. The students performed the song for their parents, along with a few poems and songs about ocean animals. Afterward, the students were able to show their parents the things they learned about ocean animals, work with their parent to create an art project, and enjoy pizza. This became my favorite way to wrap up the school year and thank the parents for their involvement.

Arrrrrg! Pirate Day!

My hope is that each year I connect with parents and leave a lasting impression on them as well. I want to be remembered as a teacher who made a difference in her student's lives and helped build them up for future success.

FANTASTIC FOUR TAKEAWAYS

1. Remember the three Cs for parental involvement: Caring, Compassion, and Conversation.

2. Reverse your perspective when communicating with parents. What would you hear?

3. Be consistent when communicating with parents. This will increase their active participation throughout the year.

4. Parents are a valuable part of your EduHero team; utilize their talents!

4

FRIENDS, ALLIES, AND SUPPORTERS

Individually, we are one drop.
Together, we are an ocean.
—Ryunosuke Satoro

How well do you know the people around you?

Every school day we come in contact with individuals who impact our classrooms, both directly and indirectly. How do you interact with these friends and supporters? As teachers, it's easy to become focused solely on our classroom instruction and overlook our sidekicks. Think about it: What would Batman be without Robin or Alfred? It takes a village to be successful, and our school support staff, volunteers, and community stakeholders play a vital role in the process.

Friends and Colleagues

Relationships among colleagues can take on various dimensions due to the school environment created by teachers, students, volunteers, parents, administrators, and of course the school support staff. My definition for school support staff is somewhat broad in nature, as it includes cafeteria personnel, custodial workers, counselors, librarians, nurses, and office administrative staff. They all play a vital role for any successful school. It's easy to overlook the importance each one these people have in the student learning taking place on a daily basis. Over the years, I have had the opportunity to work with some of the most professional support staff, who all work hard to make their school the very best, regardless of the situation. It is important for teachers to take the time to not only meet the school's support staff but establish a relationship with them. Acknowledge them and the work they contribute to the overall success of the school; they will appreciate it!

During my tenure at Silver Shores Elementary in Miramar, Florida, I witnessed firsthand the importance of our entire

Friends, Allies, and Supporters

My best friend and teammate Tonia McDermott

My fearless teammate Jennifer Fowler

My incredible teammate Sara Peisher

school community coming together to build a highly successful school from the ground up. Silver Shores Elementary was scheduled to open its doors in July 2000, but the numerous last-minute construction delays forced the school district to postpone the opening.

New teachers had already been hired and were waiting to prepare their classrooms, and students were already assigned to their teachers. At this point, it would have been very easy for everyone involved to look for someone to blame. Instead, the district leaders, new school administration, support staff, and teachers worked together in a short, two-week window to set up and prepare portable classrooms at nearby Silver Lake Elementary. Since Silver Lake was already well over student capacity limits, adding classroom portables only created space for the students to learn. Bus transportation, car rider drop-off and pickup, cafeteria space, and dozens of other issues were still being worked out as the school year started. Many of the solutions, such as starting the school day earlier, squeezing in lunch times, and having multiple release times became the norm for everyone. Our school finally opened five months later in January 2001, which was a blessing since we could use our Christmas break to relocate and set up our new classrooms. One of the most meaningful takeaways from that experience was seeing the amount of pride and ownership regarding the new school. Everyone pitched in and helped one another. When teachers finished their rooms, they didn't go home; they went to the teacher next door and asked what they could do to help. We worked as a team, and the dedication and hard work put forth by everyone involved made a tough situation manageable and memorable.

Leaders and Allies

It can be tempting to cast those in supervisory roles as super villains in our school's story, especially if you feel your school leadership is not supportive. After all, they are usually the ones in the position to say no to requests for additional resources that aren't in the budget, ideas that don't fit the norm, or changes to already packed schedules.

EduHeroes, regardless of the challenges they face, see everyone in their school community as part of their team—including the leadership. They never entertain an us-versus-them mentality regarding their principals and assistant principals. EduHeroes provide high-quality instruction in their classroom and do their job at a consistent level of excellence. Leverage your strengths and work with your leaders to help make your school a place teachers, students, and parents are proud to call theirs. I know it isn't always easy; in fact, EduHeroes also know that sometimes it's necessary to just shut the door and teach—particularly when new curriculum isn't in the budget and the boxed curriculum isn't meeting students' needs. I've certainly taken that approach! And more than once, I've reminded myself and others that I teach students, not the curriculum.

Now, how does this approach build stronger relationships with school principals? Please understand, I have never been a principal, nor have I ever wanted to assume such a challenging position within the school. My passion and love have always been teaching. Principals and other school administrators are constantly faced with unforeseen challenges I can't imagine. My question to you, "Do you believe administrators are passionate about student learning?" From my perspective, the

Leaders are those who always empower others.
—Bill Gates

Friends, Allies, and Supporters

answer is absolutely yes. A supportive principal can make all the difference, and I've been fortunate to work for many leaders who viewed teachers as professionals and experts at their craft; however, sometimes the curriculum we are forced to use doesn't match our professional philosophy.

When I began teaching in Broward County, teachers were required to teach from a script with fidelity, and we were expected to be on the exact same page at the exact same time. I wasn't able to slow down and take the time to reteach what the students didn't get the first time. I was miserable, and my students noticed.

Teaching is an art, and the ability to teach the way I taught best was taken away from me. Each of us have strengths that allow us to shine in the classroom. The standards and learning outcomes are our guides, but we need the freedom to teach in the way we teach best. I could have continued to be miserable and just made it through the year, but I knew my students deserved more than that. I gathered some research and made an appointment with my principal, Becki Britto, to plead my case. After several Q&A sessions and informal classroom observations, Ms. Britto allowed me the opportunity to make decisions based on what I knew was best for my students. I'm not sure if she was giving me additional rope to tie a pretty bow or to hang myself, but I appreciated the opportunity she gave me to be creative and take risks.

Principals are almost always our biggest supporters, and they want their teachers to be empowered to be creative in their teaching. When we as teachers are knowledgeable about the standards and we can back it up with student achievement, most principals will allow us to unleash our superpowers.

EduHeroes

John Rudzik was my principal at Northlake Park Community School in Orlando, Florida. He was the true definition of an EduHero, and I was blessed to have the opportunity to work with such an outstanding school leader. Mr. Rudzik was a former teacher who shifted his passion from the classroom to school leadership. His passion for teaching and leading showed every day in the way he supported every aspect of the school. Mr. Rudzik's motto focused on students first, and his vision was creating a school environment conducive for greatness. From the simple gestures of greeting students every morning by name to walking around to meet teachers in their classrooms, Mr. Rudzik was always available! He far exceeded the idea of an open-door policy by basically having his office wherever it was needed in the school. Mr. Rudzik would clearly meet my motto of ENCOURAGE.

As you read this story, maybe you have faced similar challenges within your school, but the question remains: How did you handle the situation? More importantly, how will you handle the next challenge? EduHeroes should always look for solutions to everyday challenges and seek to be part of the answer. As you reflect on your current school's environment, consider how you can be a part of the solution, not the problem. Find out how you can help and make a difference. Contrary to popular belief, our school leaders are not our enemy. Invite them to be a part of your EduHero team. Just imagine how strong you will become!

Supporters and Community Advocates

EduHeroes should seek community involvement to maximize their efforts to be successful, both in their classrooms and

It takes a village to raise a child, and I choose to be an actively participating member of my village.
—Megan Davis

schoolwide. Without involvement by various organizations, it can be very difficult to reach our greatest potential. For many teachers, seeking outside community involvement can be viewed as a lower priority goal since it doesn't directly impact student learning—or does it? Teaching at both public and private schools, I have realized that community interaction and COLLABORATION can highly impact my classroom teaching. As teachers, we will always teach our students to the best of our abilities regardless of the situation or environment. I have yet to see a teacher or school with unlimited resources, so why not seek outside involvement and support? There should always be room on your EduHero Team for volunteers and community leaders. I have found in many instances that community volunteers and leaders are unaware of my classroom needs. It's my responsibility to inform them and seek their assistance! Don't forget to utilize classroom parents, along with social media connections, to reach out to the local community.

It's important to build meaningful relationships with organizations and individuals who are willing to help. Have you developed a strong network of community volunteers to help UPLIFT your class to new heights? Take the time to reach out to local businesses and organizations to let them know how much you would appreciate their support. Remember, it's the "small things" that count. Support can take the form of volunteering their time, monetary contributions, or anything that could benefit your class or school. It may be necessary to coordinate your outreach efforts with your school administration to gain some extra momentum, but that shouldn't be difficult since they are a member of your EduHero team.

During one of my classroom transformations for the Polar Express, I contacted several local movie theaters to see if one of them would allow my class to view the newly released movie for free. After several conversations and describing how the movie integrated with my classroom lesson, one theater offered a compromise. The compromise consisted of each student purchasing a kid's pack from their concessions, but admission to the movie was free. It wasn't a perfect solution, but it worked! In fact, the theater offered the deal to our entire grade level, which created a nice field trip for us. Keep in mind that community involvement can take many forms and just be appreciative of the effort being made by them. I made the point to take numerous pictures, post to our class web page, and send a thank you card to the theater management team for contributing to our lesson.

I mentioned earlier about my Gingerbread Man play and the positive impact it had on my students, their parents, and the school. It's important to say that my stage props were built by local high school drama club members, and the supplies were donated by Lowe's. The stage costumes were designed and sewn by local volunteers who loved the idea of being involved in school plays. Additionally, our PTO contributed to the recording of the play and distributing individual copies to each student and volunteer involved in the production. This shows you how powerful a team you can have just by seeking a little assistance! Don't forget to take the time to thank each and every volunteer who contributed to your event or classroom activity. Remember, the next one is just around the corner!

The popularity of crowdsourcing has become an interesting and new approach for teachers to obtain resources for their classrooms. For those who are unfamiliar with crowdsourcing, it's somewhat similar to GoFundMe for seeking funding from various people to donate. From a recent survey regarding classroom supplies and materials, teachers are personally contributing an average of $500.00 for basic materials each year. This seems extremely low to me! Teachers are constantly contributing to their classrooms throughout the year to ensure student success.

Recently, I've had the opportunity to work with DonorsChoose.org for funding professional development for teachers and administrators. It's refreshing to see the energy and effort being put forth by this organization, and others like them, to encourage educators to further enhance their skills and talents in the classroom. During this past academic year, it was exciting to see organizations team up to match donated funds to send over 200-plus teachers to one of our GYTO conferences. As EduHeroes, you should continue to seek out organizations who are wanting to make a positive impact in education and in our society as a whole. Are you aware of any organizations who are making a change to our profession? If so, let everyone know; we should all take notice and applaud their efforts!

One final note about seeking outside funding and assistance: I want to caution you to make sure your school administration is aware of these efforts to seek outside resources and funding. In fact, they may have some helpful ways to assist you in your efforts.

FANTASTIC FOUR TAKEAWAYS

1 Be proactive in gaining community involvement. Take the time to reach out.

2 Building community relationships can take time, so plant the seeds now.

3 EduHeroes find creative solutions to problems.

4 Don't underestimate the superpowers of others. Ask for help when needed.

NOTES

Section 2

HARNESSING THE POWER OF THE TEAM

YOU MAY HAVE NOTICED THAT SUPER-HEROES RARELY WORK ALONE. Sure, Ironman and Wonder Woman are amazing on their own, but when they team up with the other Avengers and Justice League members (respectively), they—and their team—became almost unstoppable. Their best chance at defeating the villains is working together. Superheroes—whether they are on the big screen or in the classroom—collaborate for success.

5

EduHeroes Assemble!

You don't inspire your teammates by showing them how amazing you are. You inspire them by showing them how amazing they are.
—Robyn Benincasa

Teaching takes a special person, one who is willing to sacrifice a huge amount of their time and energy to educate and ENCOURAGE children. We and the children we serve face a growing number of obstacles every school year. The only way we can win in this career is to work together with other EduHeroes to ensure all of our students are prepared for their future endeavors. Collaboration is a key factor for our success as educators.

Gathering (and Culling) Your Team

Take a few minutes to describe yourself as a teacher. (Be honest!)

- What are your best qualities?
- How are your relationships with your fellow teachers?
- How would they describe you as a teacher?
- How would they describe you as a colleague?
- How would you describe the teachers you work with on a daily basis?

The answers to the questions above serve as the baseline for building stronger relationships with other teachers. Once we can determine our own strengths and weaknesses in the classroom, we can work on building relationships with others who can lift us up and whom we can support. After all, we are stronger together!

Our work relationships can take on several levels, and quite often they start out and stagnate at surface-level connections. Think about it: How often do you greet someone in passing in the hallway with the rhetorical question, "How are you?" Most of the time, this question doesn't come out of sincere interest in the other person's well-being; it's just an automatic greeting.

But what if you stopped walking and genuinely asked someone that same question—and then waited for the response? I challenge you to do this. Stop, look the other person in the eye, and wait. This shows them you genuinely care about them and are truly interested.

Engage with the teachers next door, as well as with those in other grade levels. I know your response: *I don't have time!* But I ENCOURAGE you to make time. Just imagine what the school culture would be like if every teacher took this opportunity to create new relationships across the entire school. Your EduHero team would become unstoppable with so many connections and varied strengths!

Stepping out of our comfort zones isn't easy. We tend to gravitate to individuals who share the same views, ideas, and opinions. I have always thought to become a better teacher you must be willing to step back and allow different perspectives to come into view. In other words, be open to new ideas, strategies, and methodologies. Building stronger teacher-to-teacher relationships across grade levels can be a great start to opening new doors for success in your classroom.

It's important to note here that not all teacher relationships are perfect, and not all the connections you make in your school will be positive. From my experience, there are some negative relationships we have to end, or at least limit. I'm not writing a "Dear Abby" column here, but I do want to caution you that it may be necessary for you to limit your association with negative individuals. Negativity is a major drain on an EduHero's superpowers, not unlike kryptonite for Superman. It can be extremely challenging to make a positive impact on students' lives if you let negativity pull you down.

Just as building positive relationships with other teachers is essential for your success, knowing when to step away from negative relationships is just as important. If you have tried numerous times to encourage a teacher who seems to live in a constant state of negativity, move forward and move on! You can't have a positive life if you surround yourself with negative people. Always be the positive influence in every relationship, but know when it is time to step away.

Collaborate to Grow

It has been a blessing for me to have the opportunity to talk with thousands of teachers each year and listen to their accomplishments and challenges. One of the most common topics of discussion stems from the lack of collaboration and sharing by fellow teachers. For some reason, many teachers tend to narrow their focus on their own classroom with little collaboration or thought for the teacher and students next door.

Have you been in a situation where teaching becomes a competition? I have experienced first- hand the challenges of others creating an environment of competition while losing focus on the most important aspect of teaching, our students. Competition creates winners and losers among teachers, while collaboration uplifts and ENCOURAGES everyone. Don't misunderstand me, healthy competition in sports and other similar settings is great, but educators should never view teaching as a sporting event.

Maybe you can relate. You may even believe that your classroom focus is justified because of time and energy limitations. If that's the case, stop and ask yourself, "What is my goal? Do I care about the success of my students, or do I care about the success of all students?"

When I taught at NorthLake Park Community School, our teacher mailboxes were centrally located cubbies. All teachers and support staff had to walk by them to get to the office. A favorite pastime was to look and see if anyone had been "Wonged." What does that mean? Being "Wonged" meant that a teacher's observation didn't go as planned and our principal John Rudzic gifted this unlucky individual with *The First Days of School: How to Be an Effective Teacher* by Harry and Rosemary Wong. I'm ashamed to admit I found this amusing. Those were not my proudest moments, and they certainly didn't fit the definition of an EduHero. We don't rise to the top by letting others sink to the bottom. An EduHero would have gone to the teacher who had the misfortune of being "Wonged" and offered assistance. If we are going to be EduHeroes for all students, we can't operate with a fend-for-yourself approach. Our collective students' long-term success will benefit when we develop collaborative relationships with fellow teachers.

I've often been asked, "But why should I share my ideas and strategies with other teachers who do not share my enthusiasm and passion for teaching?" My answer is two-fold: First, start by focusing on building relationships. It is important for us to remember not to pass judgment on other teachers simply because we feel they do not share the same passion for teaching. We all have different strengths, and we come to school with diverse back stories. That diversity means our passion will show

We don't rise to the top by letting others sink to the bottom.

up in different and unexpected ways. When you take time to get to know the teachers in your school, you may discover they are more willing to collaborate than you think. Second, if you find yourself in a school where other teachers don't share, share anyway. When you reach out, your example challenges those around you to stretch and grow. Sharing ideas and collaborating helps to develop the passion and excitement in all of us. That's how we create a school culture that benefits all students.

Rethinking Collaboration

During the summer of 2007, I accepted a kindergarten teaching position at Quail Run Elementary (QRE) in Warner Robins, Georgia. My family had recently moved from Orlando, where I had taught for several years at Northlake Park Community School. I had built a strong relationship with my kindergarten team and school administration during that time and was dragging my feet all the way up Interstate 75 to Warner Robins. Transitions and relocations can be difficult for anyone, and I found myself having to rethink my focus on collaboration. My new kindergarten team at QRE was different from my previous team, but not in a bad way—just different. The kindergarten team at my new school had worked together for a long time. They had a certain way of doing things and had established approaches that worked for them. My tendencies leaned toward teaching outside the box and trying new things in the classroom, and I was worried about how that would be received. It would have been easier for me to shut my door and teach, but I believed then, as I do now, that collaboration is the best approach to teaching.

At each teacher planning meeting at QRE, we shared our ideas and strategies with one another and pushed forward together. One of these meetings changed my life forever.

Teachers Pay Teachers (TPT) is an open marketplace for teachers and others to share and sell their instructional materials for use in the classroom. My initial introduction to TPT came from one of my QRE kindergarten team members, Lisa Brewer, during one of our weekly meetings back in early 2008. She suggested I sell my instructional materials on the site, which was not well-known at the time. After a little research on TPT's founder, former fifth-grade teacher Paul Edelman, I decided to upload a few teacher resources to the site. My initial sales for 2008 were around $300, which may have seemed low for some, but I was happy to have any supplemental income to help with bills. Fast forward into 2010, when my teacher resources on the TPT site had gained in popularity and my earnings had increased as a result. More important to me was the knowledge and pride I felt knowing I was helping teachers all over the world succeed in their classrooms.

Each year, my TPT sales continued to climb, and in September 2012, my total earnings exceeded one million dollars. Through the efforts of Paul and his small group of employees at TPT, this accomplishment hit mainstream media, and I was dubbed the "Millionaire Teacher." The instant fame made me uneasy to say the least. As a kindergarten and first-grade teacher, being interviewed on television, radio, and magazine interviews was completely out of my comfort zone. But there I was being called a "millionaire teacher" during interviews on CNN, *CBS This Morning*, and *The Steve Harvey Show* and other media outlets.

CBS This Morning

CNN Interview

The Steve Harvey Show

To be honest, the experience gave me a new perspective on how the general public views teachers and our profession. As teachers, we take pride in our abilities and efforts to help children reach their fullest potential, but not all people see our profession in the same light. It was shocking to see the number of negative comments about the teaching profession and the lack of respect given to educators who work hard every day to make a difference.

It can be an uphill battle to change public opinion. Looking back on my experience in the media spotlight, I appreciate the opportunity to communicate to others just how dedicated teachers are to their profession. With all the negativity out there today, it's important for us to uplift one another and be the positive influence to everyone around us. Take the time to compliment others around you; teaching is not a competition! From time to time, we all need positive reinforcement and encouragement from others around us. Be the EduHero who cheers others on to be their best.

The biggest lesson I have taken away from experiences at QRE and TPT is that sharing and collaboration are vital for classroom success and teacher growth. What if I had taken the approach to just shut my door and teach? What if I didn't believe so strongly in the importance of collaborating and sharing? I would not have the same life or career today had I not received the encouragement from Lisa and other educators to share my classroom resources and materials.

If you are feeling disappointed because your team lacks cohesiveness, take the lead! You can be the positive influence. Start by inviting your team to plan and create lessons together. You can also reach out to other teachers around the world through

It's important for us to uplift one another and be the positive influence to everyone around us.

My friend and collaborator Deedee Wills

social media and find like-minded people with whom you can share ideas. My friend and colleague Deedee Wills and I created a Facebook group, The Primary Collaborative. This is a group for primary grade teachers to share ideas and encourage one another. We would love to have you join us! If you teach upper grades, find a group or start your own. We are better together!

My challenge for you is to create your own EduHero Team. How well do you know the teacher next door? It's important for each of your team members to find their own strengths and powers. Everyone has the ability to contribute and build the team up to new heights; it just takes time and patience. Remember, not every idea or strategy will work in the classroom, and not all teachers are the same, but creating the environment for open communication and contribution among your fellow EduHeroes will help build a powerful team.

FANTASTIC FOUR TAKEAWAYS

1 Collaboration with others is a powerful force for grade-level success.

2 Gather your EduHero Team! You will be amazed at the positive influence being made within your school.

3 Open communication and dialogue are cornerstones for building strong collaborative schools, so make it happen.

4 Take the lead! Offer your assistance and support to others.

NOTES

Section 3

UNLEASHING YOUR EduHero POWERS

IN ANY SUPERHERO STORY, the transformation from an ordinary person to one with superhuman abilities is an important part of the narrative. One day they are average people who seem to be constantly running uphill and struggling to overcome daily challenges, and then something happens to change all that. Sometimes it's accidental and external—a spider bite or laboratory accident, for example. Other times, a life-changing event or realization brings about fantastic change.

Well, insect bites and accidental explosions aside, our EduHero powers can appear just as suddenly as any superhero's, and they require development and practice to make the most of them. With the powers already within you just waiting to be unleashed, you have the ability to make a huge impact on the people around you.

What are your EduHero superpowers? Can you encourage, motivate, inspire, uplift, engage, collaborate, nurture, and empower others around you?

The secret to unleashing these or any other EduHero powers is simple: You just need to try! It doesn't take a superhero to be a hero to others. It just takes the right attitude and a willingness to do your very best. Having the right mindset and the ability to push through those difficult and challenging times will help you uplift others. As teachers, we can be surrounded by negativity, but I encourage you to rise above it and unleash those positive powers! You will be amazed at the number of people who gravitate to you, simply because of your positive energy.

You may doubt that a positive outlook and attitude is enough to deal with the daily challenges facing you in the classroom, but let me tell you—it's a great first step in the right direction! I know you have the inner strength to overcome any obstacle that gets in your way, so that means you have what it takes to be an EduHero!

It doesn't take a superhero to be a hero to others.

6

WHAT CHANGES WILL HELP YOUR STUDENTS THRIVE?

I am enough of a realist to understand that I can't reach every child, but I am more of an optimist to get up every morning and try.
—Preston Morgan

Your primary mission is to protect and serve your students. We've already discussed how essential relationships are to that mission. So let's take the next steps now with instruction and classroom management strategies that can help your students thrive.

Leaping over Curriculum Hurdles

Do you ever feel stuck or struggle with any of the following questions?

- What would be gained by trying something new?
- What will happen if my students don't comprehend the material in a different way?
- Will the parents understand my approach and methodology to helping their child learn?
- If my grade-level team doesn't agree with my different approach, will we be able to move forward together and work as a team?
- If the school administration questions my strategies, will I be able to communicate to them the pedagogy being used to meet (and exceed) the standards?

Every fire starts with just a single spark. Every change occurs because someone dared to try something new.

If you are ready to light that spark and try something new, here's a teaching philosophy I've used that will help you strengthen your EduHero powers. It is called "Create the How and Explain the Why." This approach focuses on the ability to develop teaching strategies that meet your students' needs right where they are today.

Every fire starts with just a single spark. Every change occurs because someone dared to try something new.

Getting creative in the classroom with Kaylee and Britni

I am consistently approached at conferences by wonderful teachers who are struggling to integrate new resources and strategies into their everyday teaching. Many of them are frustrated with boxed curriculum that doesn't allow for adjustments or modifications in the classroom. I understand their frustrations; lockstep approaches don't always work for students who need a more individualized path to learning. They have an idea for a way to teach that would better serve their students but wonder how to get past the obstacle of prescribed, boxed curriculum. Here's my strategy:

1. Research best practices that are similar to your ideas and get a good understanding of the teaching strategies being discussed by subject area experts.
2. Compare your ideas and strategies with some of these best practices.
3. Ask, "Do the research and methodology of the best practices closely align with my own ideas and strategies?" If so, great!

If not, consider what you may need to change.

4. Based upon your comparisons, can you verbalize why your strategies would be successful in the classroom? Remember, prior research is important!

5. You may find there are numerous strategies and approaches that will help with curriculum development and modifications. EduHeroes are lifelong learners, so we must be willing to make changes that best meet our students' needs.

6. Take the opportunity to compare the boxed curriculum with your newly created lessons. Are you able to describe the similarities and differences between the two?

7. Once you feel confident with your lessons, discuss your approach with members of your EduHero Team. It's great to get feedback!

8. Go ahead and move forward. Make that appointment to discuss it with your school administrator. With all the research and evaluations you've conducted, it may feel like you are building a case to present in a court of law, but that's okay. Your supporting evidence will give you the confidence to discuss the rationale behind your strategies.

9. Be prepared to teach a mini-lesson to help explain and demonstrate your ideas.

I know you may be thinking that this sounds like a great deal of effort to integrate new strategies into the boxed-curriculum approach, but it's worth it! Knowing you are *uplifting* your students with new and creative ideas and strategies will feel great. School administrators, fellow teachers, and parents will appreciate your efforts, since it will ultimately benefit students.

Bringing Peace to the Classroom

There are a few other areas we should examine to help with unleashing our EduHero powers. One of these areas is effective classroom management. If used consistently, meaningful and intentional classroom management skills can create a dynamic learning environment for your students. How do you feel about your classroom management skills? Can they be improved? From my perspective, we all have room for improvement regardless of our years of teaching. The following are a few strategies that have helped me effectively manage my classroom. Please keep in mind, my experiences focus mainly on primary grades.

Call and Response

Have you ever been in a classroom where a teacher is constantly raising her voice to quiet down her students or turning on and off the lights to get their attention? From my experience, students will usually tune out these gestures over time, and the initial effectiveness will be lost. Students have a tendency to be very active and sometimes rather loud in my classroom. I have never had a quiet room due to my approach of active learning throughout the day. The question arises: "How do we keep our students actively engaged and focused on the lesson, while maintaining some form of classroom order?" My simple answer is to incorporate call and response attention-getters in your daily teaching strategies. These can make a world of difference, while allowing your students to stay on task. Here are a few of my favorite attention-getters:
- Flat Tire!
- Focus Up!

- Can I Get a Woop Woop?
- All Set? You Bet!
- Peanut, Peanut Butter and Jelly!

It would be difficult (and somewhat lengthy) for me to explain these calls and responses in detail, but I invite you to visit my YouTube channel and view myself and fellow teachers showing how these attention-getters can work for you.

 Find me on YouTube at bit.ly/djcallouts

Music Soothes the Soul

Consider incorporating music and songs into your classroom management activities. I love starting every morning with an uplifting song to start our day. Please understand, I am not a singer or musician, but that doesn't seem to matter to my students, so I don't let it bother me!

Student participation and active listening can increase dramatically when you provide engaging and fun activities like singing. When you are teaching new or difficult content, music makes the information easier to remember. Create or find tunes that can be modified to fit your classroom theme or lesson content; for example, I have created several songs to the melodies and beats of several 80s and 90s rock songs. It would be a huge stretch to think my students would recognize the tunes, but customizing the words to fit with my lessons seems to work well. I catch my students humming the tune all week long.

FANTASTIC FOUR TAKEAWAYS

1 Unleashing your EduHero powers are simple. Just try!

2 Have confidence in your abilities—you're a great teacher!

3 Don't limit your powers by negative thoughts and questions.

4 Use creative ways to manage and engage your students.

7

EDUHEROES PREPARE FOR GREATNESS

Guard your time fiercely. Be generous
with it, but be intentional about it.
—David duChemin

Are you a teacher who gets excited about the new school year?

I have always felt a sense of excitement planning for the new academic year, although it seems that it comes earlier each year! I would highly recommend you "do your work early" and get your classroom organized as soon as possible. Preparation will help with your balancing act. I know it can feel like "crunch time" right before the school year starts with planning meetings, in-service training and large amounts of paperwork, but taking the time to organize and decorate your classroom can be FUN! An organized, functional classroom is a must. Who could pass up the opportunity to shop at Target's Dollar Spot or The Dollar Tree for those must-have classroom items? This is your opportunity to "set the stage" for your students while getting prepared for the new year, but make sure you also set aside time to organize and prepare your instructional focus. Again, this can help tremendously with your balancing act: Be prepared!

Create Your Curriculum Map

One of the best ways to prepare your instructional focus is curriculum mapping. Curriculum mapping is the process of aligning learning standards and teaching. They serve as a guide to help teachers keep track of when and how the lessons will be taught. Think of it as an itinerary. If you were going on a sightseeing trip, you would probably plan out what you will be doing each day. What will you see? What will you do? How will you get there? Those are the kinds of questions a curriculum map will answer.

Curriculum maps work best when they are collaborative and flexible. Working with your EduHero team to plan out your grade level's yearlong curriculum map ahead of time will not only save you time in the long run, but it will also ensure that things are taught in a systematic, meaningful way with no gaps in the learning. So how do you get started?

- Grab your grade-level standards, a pack of colorful sticky notes, and schedule a place for your team to meet.
- During the first meeting, use the standards and sticky notes to map out the sequence for the lessons.
- After you've mapped out the sequence of the lessons, plan another meeting where you can go back and add in the materials you are going to use and how you plan to teach each lesson.

Each teacher has a different style and approach, so the second part may look a little different from teacher to teacher.

Wait! I already have a boxed curriculum, and I just follow that exactly as it's written. Okay, I hear you, but I have never found a boxed curriculum that adequately met the needs of all my students. You know your school dynamics, and only you can design a plan that best meets those needs. Taking the time to develop a curriculum map with your team will set the tone for planning and collaborating as a team. It will also save you hours of planning time throughout the year because you already have your itinerary in place. This plan gives you the freedom to enjoy the learning journey with the knowledge that your lessons are intentional and meet the learning styles and needs of your students. Remember: An EduHero must be flexible and observant. If your students need more time to learn the material, adjust accordingly.

Schedule Time for You

People outside of education do not truly understand that we *live* our careers. Teaching is a lifestyle, not just a job we can leave at the office. So how do we balance our careers and personal lives while still giving the attention needed to lead our students to greatness?

During my third year of teaching at Summerfield Elementary in Riverview, Florida, I realized my balancing act was not working well for me. My passion for teaching has always been very strong. I have the tendency to push myself to step outside the box by integrating room transformations to maximize the engagement and learning taking place in my classroom. I want kids to be excited about coming to school, and I want them to love learning. To reach these goals early in my career, I spent huge amounts of time planning, prepping, and creating lessons and materials to use in the classroom. Additionally, several fellow teachers felt the same passion and worked right alongside me (regardless of the time of day) to get the work done.

Before I knew it, my evenings and weekends became filled with creating new lessons and activities to be implemented in my classroom as soon as possible. Although this was fulfilling my passion for teaching, it created a shortfall in my personal life. At the time, all three of my children, Britni, Taylor, and Hunter, were under the age of ten. My husband, Ed, worked full time as a professor and attended post-graduate school. Many days felt like a three-ring circus as we tried to balance our family activities and teaching schedules. Needless to say, something had to give! As with any addiction, recognition was the first step. I had a teaching addiction!

Don't let what's happening around you get inside you and weigh you down.
—Anonymous

Planning and scheduling both at-school and at-home activities became the solution to help with my balancing act. Have you considered developing a personal schedule for yourself to set aside allotted time for non-work-related activities? Think about it: We have very rigid schedules for our classes, so why not create your own personal schedule to help with the balancing act? Within your plan, schedule time for yourself and family—and do not feel guilty for doing so!

As with teaching, scheduling time for yourself must be intentional and meaningful. You may not have large amounts of time or energy left after a full day of teaching, but quality over quantity applies in this situation. You must allow yourself the opportunity to relax and recharge your superpowers, since tomorrow is right around the corner!

Wherever you are in your day, be there. Keeping a leave-it-at-the-door mentality will allow you to focus on the most important things wherever you are. In the morning, when you walk through your classroom door, make a point of tuning out the outside world so you can focus on your students. Put your cellphone in your desk drawer, take a deep breath, and engage your EduHero powers. As you leave school at the end of the day, shut your classroom door and mentally switch gears to allow time for yourself and others. I know this can be challenging at times to mentally click on and off your thoughts, but you must be able to balance both sides of your life. Remember, you're in it for the long haul, and you must keep balance in your life in order to avoid burnout. We will discuss some other helpful strategies later in the chapter titled "Protect Your Superpowers," so let's keep moving forward.

FANTASTIC FOUR TAKEAWAYS

1 Get organized. The more organized you are, the more efficient you are.

2 Find time to fit everything in. Think about your daily schedule. Ask yourself, "Which parts of the day make the biggest impact?" and "Are there things I should eliminate or shorten?"

3 Be intentional with your planning time. Make a list and prioritize.

4 Choose one or two days a week to go in early or stay late. Giving yourself this time will hopefully keep you from having to take work home. To avoid burnout, evening and weekends should be spent with family and friends.

NOTES

8

EDUHEROES ARE ARTISTS

The best teachers are artists who
know the science of teaching.
–Richard Bankert

In recent years, there has been much debate as to whether teaching is an art or a science. Honestly, I think the answer is both.

Teaching is a science because it involves understanding the research about best practices, collecting and analyzing data, and experimenting with new strategies and techniques to see what does or doesn't work. It's important for us to use the research and our data to create a learning environment that will enhance and nurture student learning.

Teaching is also an art. Every classroom is different and unique in its own way. I have learned an important lesson year after year that we must reexamine our strategies and approaches to teaching. It can take various forms of creativity, imagination, and patience to reach your students on a meaningful level. It takes great skill to know the right questions to ask, when to let students persevere, and when to help.

Teaching is an art and a science because we learn from our failures and mistakes. We use what we learn and change things up and try again. One basic question we should ask ourselves: "How do we make sure we are reaching and engaging the students in our classroom?"

Use Room Transformations to Engage

One strategy I love to incorporate when it comes to engaging students in the learning process is classroom transformations. From a visual and experiential perspective, these room transformations can provide an unbelievable environment for learning to take place. If you need a great way to review or introduce difficult content, try a room transformation! It brings a unique and different setting for the classroom. Researchers have found that novelty releases neuromodulators in the brain that increase student engagement and activate learning .

My very first room transformation was in 2001, when I transformed my room into a rain forest. After collecting some ideas from *Mailbox Magazine* (I'm telling my age here) and other resources, I used carpet rolls, paper grocery bags, an umbrella, and bulletin board paper to create trees and the layers of the rain forest. The students made the animals as we learned about them and helped place them where they belonged in the rain forest. I created learning stations for the students to complete hands-on activities related to what we had been learning. Students moved from station to station gathering information and completing tasks that helped them practice and master the various skills. It wasn't perfect, but it met my expectations to enhance the student learning process, and, more importantly, the students *had fun while learning!*

Rain Forest 2001

Here are a few suggestions when planning your room transformations:

- Don't overdo it! I recommend four to five transformations a year. This will create a sense of novelty while controlling costs and allocation of time.
- Focus on specific activities that allow students opportunities to comprehend and apply the material on a deeper and more meaningful level.
- Get creative and experiment with different themes and activities. Room transformations should be based on your students' interests.
- Visit other teachers' websites for ideas. There's no need to reinvent the wheel. Find ideas that work for you, then adapt them to meet your learning goals.
- Balance the form and function of room transformations. In other words, make sure to include specific learning activities that are rigorous and challenge the student to complete the given tasks. Room transformations are great tools for enhancing student learning, but we must ensure that measurable outcomes are associated with the creative designs we use.
- As you brainstorm your room transformation ideas, take the opportunity to involve your EduHero team. Imagine transforming four or five rooms using the same theme, but with different student stations. Having students travel from room to room, completing different activities, would surely create a great learning environment. Talk it over with your team and give it a try! I would love to see pictures and videos of these team efforts.

Principal Dr. Don Royal helped us out with a lesson

- When it's all over, take the opportunity to evaluate your room transformation and make note of what you want to repeat and what you want to do differently next time.

Set the stage for your room transformations by creating a sense of excitement. Your enthusiasm will be contagious! I love to create anticipation for the lesson by giving my students some small, but special, hints leading up to the room transformation and activities. It's also fun to involve them in the process; for example, I had the students create all of the animals we used in our rain forest transformation.

While you're creating a buzz in your classroom, take an opportunity to invite other members of your extended EduHero team to your room transformations. Administrators enjoy the opportunity to see the learning taking place in your classroom firsthand. Let them be a part of the process, rather than just observers.

EduHeroes

Dino Day Room Transformation

Students love learning about dinosaurs! The Friday prior to starting the unit, I build excitement by displaying a large papier-mâché egg about the size of an extra-large balloon. It's off-white in color with some dirt rubbed on it for added authenticity since it's a dinosaur egg! I place the egg on an upper shelf in the classroom with no mention of it to the students. I want them to notice it on their own. Once the egg has been spotted, the questions begin to fly! I explain to them that the egg was dug up by my dog Zoey, and I brought it to school for everyone to see. The whole time, I'm setting the stage for our upcoming science unit the following week. I give my students clues about what type of egg it is, and they make inferences based on the clues. You might have to bite your tongue when they guess a chicken, pig, or elephant egg; remember, no laughing!

When my students go to specials, I carefully crack open the paper egg and place inside it a relatively real-looking stuffed dinosaur I purchased from Universal Studios a few

years back. Of course, my students won't think it's a real dinosaur. That would be crazy, but it sets the stage and gets them excited for the upcoming unit. When my students return to class, they all notice the cracked egg and dinosaur sitting high on the shelf. I love their initial reactions to seeing the dinosaur. This is the perfect way to get the students excited and engaged. After we've spent a week learning about dinosaurs, we have our Dino-Dig day, which gives the students the opportunity to be paleontologists for the day and excavate dinosaur bones.

To transform my classroom into a Dino-Dig Site, I purchase wooden model kits of dinosaurs from Amazon and cover them in Play-Doh. Once the Play-Doh dries, I place the pieces in a large plastic tub and cover the pieces with sand. The paleontologists will dig up the dinosaur bones and use tools to clean them off. They will examine the dinosaur pieces to figure out what type of dinosaur the bones belong to. Once we've sorted the pieces into the two different dinosaur types, we get to work putting the models together. Next, the students use nonstandard units of measurement to measure life-sized dinosaur tracks.

A teacher's canvas may look different from that of a traditional artist, but what a beautiful picture we have the opportunity to paint.

Room transformations can help tremendously with classroom management and behavior. If you feel your students aren't focusing on each station activity, take the time to re-emphasize the learning objectives and the importance for each of them to actively participate. Keep them on task and monitor their progress. I have always been pleasantly surprised with the learning taking place on these days.

Are there other ways to integrate an artistic touch to your classroom? Absolutely! I love room transformations, but they aren't the only way to bring novelty and excitement. You can

An animated read-aloud

do that in a variety of ways. One of my favorite things to do in my classroom is to have animated read-alouds. I do my very best to read the story with three, four, or five different voices to match the book illustrations and character portrayals. I love seeing my students so actively engaged, listening to the story. For many students, book readings (especially when done with a creative touch) are not part of their daily routines. Teachers should make the effort to demonstrate how enjoyable reading a book can be, and this is easily accomplished through read-alouds. If you haven't attempted to read using a more artistic and creative way, I would suggest you step outside your comfort zone and give it a try!

A teacher's canvas may look different from that of a traditional artist, but what a beautiful picture we have the opportunity to paint.

FANTASTIC FOUR TAKEAWAYS

1 We are all artists in our own way! Just give it a try.

2 Use your classroom as an art studio. Create your own masterpieces!

3 Allow your students the opportunity to be creative and use their imaginations.

4 Room transformations are a fun way to enhance the learning taking place in your class.

NOTES

9

EDUHEROES TAKE RISKS

Do not fear failure, but instead be
terrified of regret.
—Deshauna Barber, Miss USA

Do you consider yourself a risk-taker in your classroom?

How about outside your classroom? I believe we each have different natural capacities for risk. For me, the more confident I am about an idea, the greater risks I'm willing to take to bring it to life. I do want to clarify that I'm not a daredevil, so don't ask me to go bungee jumping or skydiving with you! But as an EduHero, I know we must be willing to take risks and step outside our comfort zones.

Experience has taught me that creativity stems from trying new things and not being overly concerned with failure. Be bold enough to experiment, and be intentional about learning from successes and failures. I cannot count the number of times my great ideas didn't turn out according to plan! But I always learn something.

In 2014, I had been trying to balance my teaching schedule while traveling around the country presenting at various teacher conferences, along with creating new materials on Teachers Pay Teachers—and let's not forget time for my personal life. I felt my balancing act was tilted greatly with need for major leveling! My husband, Ed, picked me up from the airport after a long flight from Los Angeles back to Orlando and suggested I host my own conference to slow down the amount of traveling I was doing with conference presentations. My first reaction was no way was I going to take the risk of creating my own conference! My first thoughts were all about the what ifs that could go wrong, like *what if no one showed up to the conference? What if my message isn't received well?*

It's easy to focus on the possible negative outcomes versus the possible positive results from taking risks. As terrified as I was, Ed

We all need people who will cheer us on and ENCOURAGE us to reach past our comfort zones.

was not willing to accept no as an answer, and he moved forward with planning a one-day workshop in Orlando. Before I knew it, he had a date scheduled along with a location at the Florida Mall and Conference Center. At that point, I realized he was dead serious about me hosting my own conference. I quickly worked on a conference name, "Ready, Set, Teach," and outlined a tentative one-day schedule. We had one conference room that would hold

"Ready, Set, Teach!" Taking a leap of faith with our first conference!

approximately one hundred attendees, which seemed like a large number at that time. Well, to sum it up rather quickly, we sold out the conference, and I had the opportunity to meet some wonderful teachers. In hindsight, I'm not sure why I was so nervous to start this new venture, but I am glad Ed didn't accept my fear of failure as an excuse not to try something new. That first conference paved the way for Get Your Teach On, which has been wildly successful, thanks to so many amazing educators.

The biggest takeaway I hope you get from this story is the importance to push past the negative thoughts. We all need people who will cheer us on and ENCOURAGE us to reach past our comfort zones, so let me be that person for you right now. If you are afraid of doing something new because you might fail, I want to encourage you to turn your thoughts around and ask: "How will I handle the success of my efforts?"

Have you tried any new things lately? Were they successful? Have you encouraged others around you to stretch their comfort zones? Do you ask your students to take risks in the classroom? As EduHeroes, you should provide your students with the confidence to take risks and stretch their comfort zones. You will be amazed by your students' improvement when you create an environment conducive for taking risks in the learning process. Just remember, your students must trust you and know you have their backs if they fail at something. Help them get back up, dust them off, and keep the learning going!

FANTASTIC FOUR TAKEAWAYS

1 Don't forget: Risks are just successes waiting to happen!

2 Focus on your accomplishments and use any failure as a lifelong lesson for future success.

3 Our comfort zones are only defined by us; stretch your zone!

4 Make sure to ENCOURAGE and applaud successes. Be the cheerleader for yourself and others!

10

EDUHEROES ARE LIFELONG LEARNERS

Never stop learning, because life never stops teaching.
—Anonymous

The fact that teachers are leaving the profession at an alarming rate affirms that teaching is not for the faint of heart.

This career requires a dedicated commitment to positively impacting children's lives. Since we are such dedicated professionals, we will face times when our creative juices are drained. Talking to and collaborating with other dedicated educators can help us refuel our creativity and re-energize our spirits.

I am amazed by the long-time educators I meet at our conferences. Some have been teaching for thirty-plus years, and they are still looking for strategies to enhance their classroom learning. As educators, we should never stop learning or looking for ways to improve. But during my early years of teaching, I found it challenging to find time to read professional development books or attend conferences. My focus was survival!

Things finally changed for me when I found my deepest passion in the classroom: reading. My passion for reading and early childhood literacy led me to research and read anything relating to the subject. I could not stop searching for best practices and strategies for enhancing my classroom teaching. I truly enjoyed developing lessons to enhance my students' learning.

When I started looking for resources, I was astounded by the wealth of ideas available—and the depth and breadth of educational resources have only increased in recent years. Because time is one of our most limited resources during the school year, making the most of technology and online learning resources can enhance our classroom teaching and learning. Please understand, not all online resources are beneficial for professional development. Be careful not to go down a rabbit hole and lose track of the purpose for your search in the first place. I cannot count the number of times my online search ended virtual miles away from my intended goal. Again, we have to be intentional with our time and objectives and stay on task when we're online.

On a positive note, there are so many great websites, blogs, chat rooms, and other social media sites that create virtual learning platforms for sharing ideas and experiences with other educators. That means you don't have to dream up every idea or strategy you use in your classroom. Take what you learn from others and make it your own! What's important is that you fully understand the theory behind a strategy to ensure that 1) it has the intended effect, and 2) it meets your learning goals, meaning, and intent. (And remember to give credit to your resources; it's an education thing!)

Sharing lessons and research with others can lead to powerful collaboration. Within your school, grade-level meetings can be a great sounding board for new ideas and strategies for everything from math, science, reading, social science—you name it! Which brings me to another point: We have a wealth of knowledge and experience in the classrooms right down the

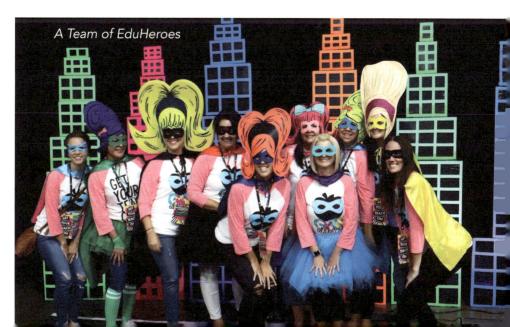

A Team of EduHeroes

hall. Think about the combined years of experience on your grade-level team. It's probably a crazy high number when you add it up! Learning from others' life experiences, hearing their stories of what worked and what didn't, can give you a perspective you may never have found on your own. I have been blessed to learn from both first-year and veteran teachers. Each have unique perspectives on teaching and learning that have proven valuable to me. Remember: You do not need to reinvent the wheel; just ask others on your EduHero team! Sharing and collaborating can save you time and energy.

Many schools have established Professional Learning Communities (PLCs) to create an open dialogue for educators to share a variety of topics for professional development. These communities provide a great opportunity to meet and discuss key takeaways and potential changes to educational practices with others who share a passion for learning. Have you recently been involved with a PLC? If not, I strongly recommend you consider joining or creating one for your grade level, or even schoolwide, to share your experiences and perspectives.

Are you a lifelong learner? Have you had the opportunity to attend a workshop, conference, in-service or a college course recently? Have you read a professional development book or article lately (And yes, this book counts!). Any time you attend a conference or read a good professional development book, I ENCOURAGE you to share your perspective on the subject with your PLC, your online learning community, or the teachers down the hall. It's great to create a dialogue and spark collaborative thinking.

FANTASTIC FOUR TAKEAWAYS

1 Find your passion and share it with others.

2 Read a book for pleasure. Read one for professional development. Share both!

3 Embrace technology. So many resources and ideas are available at your fingertips.

4 Don't forget about the wealth of knowledge and experience that surrounds you every day. Seek the advice of the educators in your school and online communities!

NOTES

BELIEVE IN YOUR EDUHERO POWERS

Working hard is important, but there is something that matters even more: believing in yourself.
—Harry Potter

As you gain and strengthen your EduHero powers, it's important to share them with others.

Sometimes we are hesitant to show off our newly found abilities, especially if they have not been tested before. For example, during a classroom observation have you introduced a brand-new strategy you've never used before, or did you stick with a more familiar, time-tested one? Usually, we fall back on familiarity to avoid unpredictable outcomes with our students. This isn't a bad thing—just a matter of confidence and comfort level! As we discussed earlier, when building your EduHero team, keep in mind your own abilities, but don't forget to utilize the strengths of others around you. Remember: confidence is gained by experience, but the experience doesn't have to come from you alone!

How do we build confidence in our abilities as teachers? Is it based on student test scores, feedback from parents, other teachers, or administrators? To be effective teachers, we need positive constructive feedback to improve our teaching abilities. We are lifelong learners, right? The challenge: How do we play to our strengths while working on improving our weaknesses?

Take the time to write down your strengths. Make sure to include your weaknesses as well because it's important to realize areas where you still need to learn and grow. Again, stay positive and don't be overly critical of yourself. This list is a great starting point for building confidence in your own abilities and attributes. I want to caution you not to compare yourself to other teachers around you. Focus on what makes you unique! If you asked other members of your EduHero team, do you think their list would be similar to yours or completely different? If you

Remember: confidence is gained by experience, but the experience doesn't have to come from you alone!

haven't noticed in most superhero movies, every superhero has unique and different powers from others around them. I believe this is a deeper revelation into the importance of diversity and teamwork rather than just a coincidence!

After you have created your list of strengths and weaknesses, can you provide some examples that further highlight your teaching abilities? For example, my personal list of strengths includes:

- Passion for teaching
- Sharing with others
- Caring for my students, both in and out of class
- Reading and exploring teaching strategies for the classroom
- Complimenting others and lifting them up

As I mentioned earlier, reading and literacy are my jam! It's been a passion for me for a long time, and it has become one of my best strengths in the classroom and presenting at conferences around the country. If you ever want to strike up a conversation with me, just mention the topic of reading and literacy; you will probably have to make an excuse to get away from me! I have become a subject matter expert in this area and continuously work hard to share my insights with others. Please understand, I'm not boasting; this topic is a strength for me. From your list of strengths, do you feel you have mastered certain abilities? If so, please share with others. On the flip side, make sure to recognize other teachers' strengths and seek their insights and guidance as well.

Now on to my weaknesses. Personally, I have found several items on my list that make me work harder to improve year after year. One of my major weaknesses is that I am not a morning person. Let me reiterate this one—I am not a morning person! This can be challenging since school starts before 8:00 a.m. (Of course, 9:00 or 10:00 a.m. would be so much better!). I have always struggled with this, and it doesn't matter how much caffeine that I have; it's no help.

One of my most embarrassing and entertaining stories came when I was working at Quail Run Elementary. To set the background, my classroom was located on the far end of the school, right near the playground. The teacher parking lot was directly in front of the end doors leading to the kindergarten hallway, which made a direct path to my classroom. Boy, this made it quite easy for me to park and walk directly into my room with little effort. This scenario worked perfectly for me; I just beat the first bell, and I was home free! Well, after several nationwide events involving security issues within schools, QRE implemented stronger security measures on entering the school. Everyone had to begin entering through the main corridor during normal school hours. Of course, this was not near my classroom at all! Walking all the way to the main door and through the main hall greatly impacted this not-a-morning-person's ability to make it to my classroom before the morning bell. One morning, I was running slightly behind and realized that the end doors to the kindergarten hallway were locked since normal school hours had started. Instead of taking a walk of shame through the main entrance and past the office, I decided my best approach was to crawl through my classroom window that was facing the playground and bus stop loop. I slipped through the window rather gracefully (from my perspective) and beat the morning bell by just minutes! Impressed with my quick thinking and problem-solving skills (and thankful that I wore a long dress to work), I went about the morning with little concern. However, this sense of accomplishment was quickly dissolved during my scheduled lunch time. While standing in the cafeteria speaking with my principal Dr. Thomas, a first-grade student approached us with a concerned look on her face. She asked us if there was a problem with my classroom door, since she saw me crawl through the window earlier that morning as she was exiting the bus. You should have seen the look on my face—sheer shock and embarrassment! As I back-pedaled, I told the student there wasn't a problem but thanked her for the concern. With Dr. Thomas, I had to come clean and explain the scenario that had led to this embarrassing moment. Although it became a memorable, lasting moment, it made me take inventory of my areas for improvement.

Understanding that I struggle with early morning energy levels, it's important for me to plan for my shortcomings in this area. My solution? Before leaving at the end of the day, I make sure everything is prepared for the next day. Basically, I can walk into my classroom in the morning and be ready for my students immediately. I would rather allocate my time after school for preparation than arrive at school extra early; that's just me. That said, we are all different! Some teachers leave immediately after the final bell rings for the day. It would be easy for me to judge those teachers and assume they aren't committed to teaching or just wants to do the very minimum to get by with their students. But this probably isn't accurate; they are just planning differently and hopefully playing to their strengths. In fact, they may have been at school while I was still hitting the snooze button.

We are all different and should keep an open mind when working with others.

How do you overcome your weaknesses? How can you change these into strengths for you and your class? It's not always feasible to make dramatic changes to your style of teaching, but each of us should be continuously looking for opportunities to enhance our superpowers. I want you to be confident in your abilities and stand up for what you believe in when it comes to teaching. Be strong and lead the way for others.

FANTASTIC FOUR TAKEAWAYS

1 Know your strengths and weaknesses.

2 Play to your strengths while working on improving your weaknesses.

3 Challenge yourself to strengthen your EduHero superpowers.

4 Remember: only use your powers for good!

12

PROTECT YOUR SUPERPOWERS

In order to have a positive relationship with others, you first must have a positive relationship with yourself.
—Anonymous

The career of teaching can take its toll. As with any superhero movie, there are always difficult challenges and crazy circumstances, along with numerous battles that end with an amazingly quick recovery by both villains and superheroes. For EduHeroes, it may not be as easy as it is in the movies to bounce back from the daily challenges, so we must protect our superpowers! Sometimes it's important for us to hang up our capes at the end of the day and take the opportunity to re-energize our batteries. I know every one of us is different, but here are a few of my favorite ways to rejuvenate myself from a challenging day of teaching:

- Read a good book.
- Watch a favorite show (no binge watching).
- Spend some quality time with family and friends.
- Go Big! Enjoy the pampering of a hot stone massage.
- Go for a walk and take in the fresh air and change of scenery.
- Meet a friend for dinner or just ice cream.
- Indulge in some non-school related retail therapy.

What is your kryptonite? We all have challenges and struggles in and out of the classroom. We must be able to protect ourselves and re-energize our powers. It's important for you to find ways to relax and regain your mental and physical strength for the next day. It's impossible to give your students the attention they need if you can't first give yourself opportunities to regain your energy and focus. In other words, take care of yourself!

We are all works in progress, and we must be open to both praise and criticism. Personally, my feelings can get hurt rather easily from harsh feedback, but actually it can be a soul-searching moment for self-improvement.

ENCOURAGE others and cheer for their success!

A couple of years ago after one of my Get Your Teach On (GYTO) conferences (location not given to protect the innocent bystanders), I received some rather harsh feedback from one of the attendees. It wasn't the first time presenting the material, so I was surprised that this teacher was so critical, given the large amount of information covered during the two-day conference. I had always received positive feedback from previous conferences, so I assumed that attendees were expecting sessions with heavily researched strategies and methodologies. In retrospect, maybe it was too much content in such a short period of time, but again, more is better, right? After reading (and crying a little) over the survey response, I determined the best course of action was to evaluate each session and incorporate songs, chants, and hands-on activities to ensure my presentations would inform, educate, and entertain everyone who attended GYTO in the future. In hindsight, it would have been easy to become defensive and ignore the negative comments and focus only on the positive ones, but I would not have learned from their perspective. This experience taught me to always keep in mind that it doesn't matter how much information you give out, it matters how much they take in.

Have you had this type of experience when you thought you "rocked" that well-planned classroom lesson, only to realize the dozens of blank stares from your students? Or have you experienced a classroom observation that went "sideways" rather quickly when your students lost all interest in your lesson? It happens! Stay positive and use these moments to build up your superpowers. EduHeroes must be willing to strengthen their powers through self-reflection and evaluation. Be careful not to be overly critical of yourself. It's important to set high expectations, but don't be unrealistic in your goal setting. It's hard to climb high in life when you are constantly knocking yourself down. So build yourself up and encourage the people

We are stronger together!

surrounding you. Be the positive influence, and you will see the change taking place around you.

Building strong personal and professional relationships can increase your superpowers. As EduHeroes, we should create connections with people who ENCOURAGE us to be stronger educators. Take advantage of social media to connect with teachers around the world. Can you imagine the different perspectives and insights you will have when you dialogue with a large community of educators? If you haven't already done so, join a Facebook group or create a blog or class web page to reach out and connect with others. Remember, EduHeroes are stronger together!

Don't underestimate the power of friendships in protecting your superpowers. Over the past twenty years, I have made some of the most wonderful friendships with people who share my passion for uplifting others. It is interesting to note that my friendships were formed through so many different ways, such as teacher meetups, Facebook groups, blogs, TPT, professional development conferences, and, of course, the classroom!

As you build new friendships, rekindle old ones, and enjoy your current ones, make it a point to have fun and cherish the moments. It's very easy for each of us to get caught up in the next fire to extinguish and lose perspective on the most important things in life. How often are you asked, "How long have you been teaching?" Does it surprise you the number of years you have been in the profession? For me, years fly by, but sometimes the day-to-day can feel like an eternity! So make every moment count and create those lifelong relationships. Never underestimate the power of these lasting friendships.

"Be somebody that makes everybody feel like a somebody."
—Kid President

FANTASTIC FOUR TAKEAWAYS

1 Take care of yourself every day (and don't forget to wear comfortable shoes)!

2 Find the positive moments, even during the most challenging times.

3 Build friendships that will lift you up.

4 Be the positive influence for everyone around you.

NOTES

13

MOVING FORWARD

You can't go back and change the beginning, but you can start where you are and change the ending.
—C.S. Lewis

Where do we go from here? Although this book was not intended to provide you with specific instructional or how-to strategies for teaching, hopefully it provided you with some new insights and food for thought for becoming an EduHero to everyone around you.

As you are finishing reading the book, you may be saying, "I already do these things with my students." That's great! I would like to challenge you to continue to use your EduHero powers to help uplift and strengthen the people around you. I guarantee you will become a stronger teacher!

If you are reading this towards the middle or end of the school year and you find yourself wishing you had done things differently, don't despair. It's never too late; start right where you are, today. Additionally, the good news is that each school year, we get a fresh start—a chance to learn from our mistakes, to try new things, and to start over with a brand-new group of students.

I have always loved the short story about the young boy walking the beach and repeatedly bending over and picking up one of the hundreds of starfish that washed ashore and tossing it back into the ocean. An observer asks, "Why are you throwing the starfish back into the water, since there are hundreds washed ashore and you aren't making a difference?"

The boy simply replies after tossing a starfish back into the water, "It made a difference to that one."

Isn't that our role as teachers? We make an impact, one student at a time. Sometimes it can feel overwhelming when you have twenty-plus children in your class, but you are the ENCOURAGER for your students!

Are you at a crossroads in your teaching? Have you decided on the path you are wanting to take? Remember, you are not alone. Our profession is built upon hard-working, dedicated teachers who want to ENCOURAGE others. Surround yourself with people who want the best for you and your students. Take this opportunity to go back and take a look at my motto acronym, then make one for yourself. Share it with others and transform your relationships into powerful tools for success.

I challenge each of you to become someone's hero. Your impact on students' lives can be tremendous, although you may not fully see it since you are only a small part of their lives for a short while. However, your impact can last a lifetime, as Mrs. Schmidt's kindness and caring some forty-plus years ago did with me. Remember, it's the small everyday gestures and acts of kindness that count. You make a difference. You are an EduHero, so wear your cape proudly.

Your passion can change the world, but don't let the world change your passion.

You can't go back and change the beginning, but you can start where you are and change the ending.
—C.S. Lewis

BIBLIOGRAPHY

Chapter Two

1. Marzano, Robert J. *Art and Science of Teaching/Relating to Students: It's What You Do That Counts.* Alexandria: ASCD, 2011.
2. Wong, Harry and Rosemary Wong. *The First Days of School: How to Be an Effective Teacher.* Mountain View, CA: Harry K. Wong, Publications, Inc., 1997.
3. Souers, Kristen and Pete Hall. *Fostering Resilient Learners: Strategies for Creating a Trauma-Sensitive Classroom.* Alexandria: ASCD, 2016.
4. Pierson, Rita. "Every Kid Needs a Champion." Filmed May 2013. TED Talk Video, 7:36. https://www.ted.com/talks/rita_pierson_every_kid_needs_a_champion?language=en.

Chapter Three

1. García, Lily Eskelsen and Otha Thornton. "The Enduring Importance of Parental Involvement." *NEA Today,* November 18, 2014. http://neatoday.org/2014/11/18/the-enduring-importance-of-parental-involvement-2.

ABOUT THE AUTHOR

Deanna Jump is an award-winning kindergarten teacher. She has taught kindergarten and first grade for twenty-one years and holds a master's degree in curriculum and instruction, as well as an educational specialist degree in early literacy and reading. Deanna has a true passion for creating and sharing best practices and activities that make learning fun, and she is a well-known teacher-author for the popular site Teachers Pay Teachers. Holding the number-one bestseller position, Deanna's work has been covered by CNN, Fox News, MSNBC, PBS, *CBS This Morning*, *Time Magazine*, *Bloomberg Business Week*, *Business Insider*, *Education Week*, and the popular *Steve Harvey* talk show. Deanna is the cofounder of Get Your Teach On and travels around the country to share her knowledge of a hands-on approach to teaching and learning. She is also the author of the website, *Mrs. Jump's Class*.